Laura Poliakoff

Clockwork

Methuen Drama

Published by Methuen Drama, 2012

Methuen Drama, an imprint of Bloomsbury Publishing Plc

1 3 5 7 9 10 8 6 4 2

Methuen Drama
Bloomsbury Publishing Plc
50 Bedford Square
London WC1B 3DP
www.methuendrama.com

ISBN 978 1 408 17299 5

A CIP catalogue record for this book is available from the British Library

Available in the USA from Bloomsbury Academic & Professional,
175 Fifth Avenue/3rd Floor, New York, NY 10010.
www.BloomsburyAcademicUSA.com

Typeset by Mark Heslington Ltd, Scarborough, North Yorkshire

 HighTide Festival Theatre

HighTide Festival Theatre present

CLOCKWORK

A new play by Laura Poliakoff

First performance at the HighTide Festival, Halesworth, Suffolk on 4 May 2012.

Production sponsored by AEM International.

CLOCKWORK

A world premiere by Laura Poliakoff
A HighTide Festival Theatre production

Troll Face	Rachel Atkins
Etienne	Shomarri Diaz
Mikey	Kern Falconer
Carl	Russell Floyd
Sarah	Matilda Ziegler

Director	Steven Atkinson
Design	Richard Kent
Lighting	Matt Prentice
Sound and Music	Tom Mills
Costume Supervisor	Holly White
Assistant Director	Richard Fitch
Casting	Camilla Evans CDG
Production Manager	Jae Forrester
Stage Manager	Silki D Morrison
Assistant Stage Manager	Caroline Steele

The producers would like to thank Heather Newill

CAST

RACHEL ATKINS (TROLL FACE)

Rachel trained at the Royal Welsh College of Music and Drama
Theatre credits include: *The Marriage of Figaro* (Watermill); *Design for Living* and
The Picture (Salisbury); *Mariana Pineda* (Arcola); *Villette, Snake In The Grass, Joking
Apart* (Stephen Joseph Theatre); *Murder in Paris* (Basingstoke and Windsor tour);
The Orchestra (Southwark Playhouse); *The Revenger's Tragedy* (Hen and Chickens);
The Tempest (Wales Actors, tour); *Simply Hostile* (Man in the Moon); *Snake House*
(Greenwich Studio Theatre); *No End of Blame* (Moving Being Theatre Co); *Pax*
(Chapter Arts Centre); *Son of Man* (Bute Theatre); *Race* (Sherman Theatre); *The Castle*
(Old Red Lion Theatre). Television credits include: *Tati's Hotel, Doctors, Miss Marple,
Casualty, Most Mysterious Murders, Tracey Beaker, Pompeii, Eastenders, 15 Storeys
High, Ladies and Gentlemen...Jo Brand, Dangerfield, Kiss Me Kate, Grange Hill, Stick
With Me Kid, Bringing Baby Home, The Country Girl, La la la*. Radio credits include:
Rachel plays Vicky Tucker in *The Archers* and is also a regular voice for *BBC Radio
Drama* and *BBC Radio Comedy*.

SHOMARRI DIAZ (ETIENNE)

Shomarri is 19 and from Hackney. He has been taking acting classes since a young age
and joined the profession in 2011. In this short time, he has racked up some impressive
credits including A Touch of Cloth (TV/FIlm Sky), Married to the Game (Theatre
503), Sonnett Walks (Globe) Team Spirit (Tricycle) and various short films. Shomarri is
delighted to be working with HighTide.

KERN FALCONER (MIKEY)

Theatre credits include: *The Government Inspector* (Almeida); *39 Steps* (Three UK
Tours); *Macbeth, Importance of Being Ernest* (Aquilla, New York); *The Clearing* (Stellar
Quines); *Puntilla and his Man Matti, The Hypochondriac* (Dundee Rep); *Travesties*
(Nottingham Playhouse); *Merlin, Confessions of a Justified Sinner* (Royal Lyceum
Edinburgh); *Dad's Army* (Two UK Tours); *As You Like It* (TAG); *Twelfth Night* (Brunton
Theatre).

Television credits include: *Band of Gold* (Carlton TV); *Taggart* (STV); *River City* (BBC);
Barmy Aunt Boomerang (BBC); *Strathblair* (BBC); *The Bill* (Carlton TV); *Wedding Belles*
(Channel 4). Film credits include: *The Bruce, Macbeth* (Cromwell Films); *The Butterfly
Man* (Channel 4).

RUSSELL FLOYD (CARL)

Russell's career includes theatre, musicals, television, film, pantomime and radio. Theatre includes working with RSC and National Theatre and producing theatres at Ipswich, Plymouth, Hull Truck, Cardiff, and most recently a number of new plays, alongside appearing in leading roles in tours of Europe. Television includes long-running roles Michael Rose in EastEnders (1995–2000) and DC Ken Drummond in The Bill (2001–2004). Radio drama includes working with Oliver Reed, Michael Troughton, Tom Baker and Stephen Tomkinson. Film includes playing a gangster opposite Mark McGann and John Benfield in Endgame, which premiered at Cannes. Voice-over work includes animation, where he worked with David Jason on 'The Snow Queen'. Russell has also worked as a presenter in France, Germany, USA and UK, and presented Carlton Food Network's 'Taste Today' for the BBC. In 2009 he won best actor in the Brighton Fringe awards for his portrayal of Frank in "Bullet" by Joe Penhall. Russell trained at RADA and is a devoted Crystal Palace fan.

He won Best Actor at Brighton Festival for Joe Penhall's *The Bullet* and most recently played John Ellis in *The Hangman* to great critical acclaim.

MATILDA ZIEGLER (SARAH)

Theatre: School for Scandal (Barbican); Twelfth Night (RSC); The Marquis of Keith (Gate Theatre); Mr Bean (Pola Jones Tour); Self Catering (Cockpit Theatre); Judgement Day (Old Red Lion); Crimes of the Heart (Liverpool Playhouse); As You Like It, King Lear (Oxford Stage Co); The Constant Wife, (Theatre Clywd); The Recruiting Officer (Manchester Royal Exchange); The Great Pretenders (Gate Theatre / Tour); Women Laughing (Royal Court); Inadmissible Evidence, Machinal (National Theatre); The Lady From The Sea (Lyric, Hammersmith); An Inspector Calls (Aldwych and World Tour); Volpone (Natonal Theatre); The Memory of Water, Featuring Loretta (Hampstead Theatre); Look Back In Anger (National Theatre).

Film: City Slacker (Highwire Films); Mr Bean (20th Century Fox); Decadence (dir. Steven Berkoff); Jilting Joe (Warner Sisters).

Television includes: Lewis, Lark Rise To Candleford, Outnumbered, Lead Balloon, Mr Bean, Doctors, Inspector Linley, A Small Family Business, Killing Hitler, Swiss Tony, Home, Summer in Transylvania, Holby, Against All Odds, As You Like It, Casualty, Where the Heart is, Smitten, Harbour Lights, Mr White Goes To Westminster.

Radio: Includes: Giles Wembley-Hogg Goes Off, Rigor Mortis, Mr Mulliner, The Queen's Nose, The Party Line.

COMPANY

LAURA POLIAKOFF (WRITER)
After graduating from Bristol University, Laura worked as a freelance researcher on a variety of film and TV projects. She returned to London to take up a place on the Screenwriting course at The National Film and Television School, graduating in February 2011. Scripts: *Prude* (2011), an original screenplay. Film and TV credits: *Bertie Crisp* NFTS graduation film (2011) - Laura was co-writer of 10' short animation with director Francesca Adams, starring Kathy Burke, Mark Benton and Tamsin Greig. Theatre Credits: *Pablo*, a 13' short performed at The Hen and Chickens Theatre, directed by Miriam Lucia.

STEVEN ATKINSON (DIRECTOR)
Steven is Artistic Director of HighTide Festival Theatre

Training: Read Film and Theatre at Reading University and interned at Hampstead Theatre following his graduation in 2005. He became Literary Manager of Hull Truck Theatre in 2006 and then Artistic Director of HighTide Festival Theatre in 2007. Direction for HighTide: *Incoming* by Andrew Motion (HighTide Festival 2011 / Latitude Festival, Aldeburgh Poetry Festival); *Dusk Rings A Bell* by Stephen Belber (HighTide Festival 2011, Edinburgh Festival, Watford Palace Theatre); *Lidless* by Frances Ya-Chu Cowhig (HighTide Festival 2010, Edinburgh Festival, West End); *Muhmah* by Jesse Weaver (HighTide Festival 2009) and *The Pitch* by Nick Payne (Latitude Festival). Other Direction includes: *The Afghan and the Penguin* by Michael Hastings *(BBC Radio 4)*; *Freedom Trilogy* by various (Hull Truck Theatre); *Sexual Perversity in Chicago* by David Mamet (Edinburgh Festival). Awards include: A Fringe First for *Lidless*; two SOLT Stage One Bursaries for *Lidless* and *Stovepipe*; a Whatsonstage Award nomination for Best Off-West End Production (*Stovepipe*); and Esquire's Brilliant Brits 2009.

RICHARD KENT (DESIGN)
Up coming work includes: *13* (NYMT, Apollo)

Recent work includes: *Titanic* (MAC Theatre, Belfast), *Richard II* (Donmar Warehouse), *Mixed Marriage* (Finborough Theatre), *Decline and Fall* (Old Red Lion), *Stronger and Pariah* (Arcola), *Gin and Tonic* and *Passing Trains* (Tramway, Glasgow). Richard has worked as Associate to Christopher Oram since 2008, Working on numerous shows at the Donmar *Including Spelling Bee, King Lear* (also BAM, New York), *Passion, Red* (also Broadway and Mark Taper Forum, LA 2012), *A Streetcar Named Desire* as well as *Ivanov, Twlefth Night, Madame De Sade,* (Donmar West End) and *Hamlet* (DWE, Elsinore Denmark and Broadway). Other work as associate includes *Don Giovanni* (Metropolitan Opera), *Madame Butterfly* (Houston Grand Opera) *Billy Budd* (Glyndebourne), *Company* (Sheffield Crucible), *Dantons Death* (National Theatre) *Evita* (Broadway) and the upcoming *Nozze Di Figaro* (Glyndebourne).

MATT PRENTICE (LIGHTING)

Matt started his theatre career as a trainee lighting designer and production electrician at the Bristol Old Vic Theatre Royal. After several years of freelance work as a Lighting Designer and Production Electrician, Matt joined Mountview Academy of Theatre Arts, first as a Lighting Tutor and then as Head of Lighting. In January 2006 Matt moved to the Royal Academy of Dramatic Art as Head of Lighting.

Recent freelance Lighting Design credits include: Punchdrunk and National Theatre's productions of Faust and Masque of the Red Death; Stove Pipe, HighTide in association with the National Theatre Mar 09; Ditch, HighTide and Old Vic London Production Mar 10, Lidless, High Tide and Edinburgh production and West End transfer Mar 11; Dusk Ring a Bell and Midnight Your Time at Assembly One Edinburgh and transfer of Dusk Ring a Bell to Watford Place Theatre September 2011. Matt was Best Lighting Design winner, Critics Circle Awards 2006 for the production of Faust.

TOM MILLS (SOUND)

Productions as Composer, Musical Director and Sound Designer include:
As Composer and/or Sound Designer: *The Way of the World* (Sheffield Crucible);*Boys* (HighTide, The Nuffield Theatre, Southampton, Headlong Soho Theatre); *Benefactors* (Sheffield Studio); *Huis Clos* (Donmar Warehouse at Trafalgar Studios); *Realism and Mongrel Island* (Soho); *Moonlight & Magnolia's, Great Expectations* (Watermill Theatre); *Cinderella, Aladdin* (Lyric Hammersmith); *Electra* (Gate Theatre); *A Midsummer Night's Dream, Edward Gant's Amazing Feats of Lonliness* (Headlong); *Elektra* (Young Vic); *Wittenberg, Unbroken* (Gate Theatre); *The Eternal Not* (National Theatre); *Othello* (Assembly Rooms, Bath); *Assasins* (Eyebrow Productions).

As Composer: *The Littlest Quirky* (Theatre Centre); *Dusk Rings a Bell* (Edinburgh, Watford Palace Theatre, HighTide Festival); *The Prince of Denmark* (National Theatre Discover Programme); *Dick Whittington* (and Arranger, Lyric Hammersmith); *Wanderlust* (Royal Court); *Pericles, Macbeth* (Open Air Theatre Regents Park) and he was music associate on Moscow Live, Lidless and Ditch for the 2010 HighTide Festival.

As Composer and Musical Director: *Breathing Irregular* (Gate Theatre); *Oliver Twist* (Storm on the Lawn at The Egg, Theatre Royal Bath).

As Musical Director, Composer and Sound Designer: *The Jungle Book, The Grimm Brothers' Circus* and *Metropolis* (The Egg, Theatre Royal Bath)

As Musical Director: *Kreutzer Sonata* (Gate Theatre), *Return to the Forbidden Planet* (Bath Spa Music Society); *Band of Blues Brothers* (Panthelion Productions).

RICHARD FITCH (ASSISTANT DIRECTOR)

Richard is Resident Assistant Director at HighTide Festival Theatre. He trained at LIPA and the Young Vic.

He was the 2010 recipient of the Sir Paul McCartney Human Spirit Award.

Directing includes: *Welsh Atlantis* (Latitude Festival 2012), *The Sandman* (Riverside Studios), *The Hour of Feeling* (HighTide Festival 2012), *The Boy Who Lived Down the Lane* (Riverside Studios & Yong Siew Toh Conservatory of Music, Singapore), *Unclothed* (The King's Head Theatre), *Kindertransport* (Unity Theatre, Co-Director) and *The Pillowman* (LIPA).

Assistant Directing includes: *Island* (National Theatre), *Jack and the Beanstalk* (Watford Palace Theatre), *Four Nights in Knaresborough* (Southwark Playhouse), *The Marriage of Figaro* (The Watermill Theatre), *Lakeboat* and *Prairie du Chien* (Arcola Theatre), *The Machine Gunners* (Polka Theatre), *Double Falsehood* (The Union Theatre & New Players Theatre), *The Captive* (Finborough Theatre), *The Great British Country Fete* (UK Tour, The Bush Theatre & Latitude).

Richard has assisted workshops at the NT Studio and Young Vic. He is Visiting Director at LIPA.

CAMILLA EVANS CDG (CASTING DIRECTOR)

Theatre: *Boys* (HighTide Festival 2012), *Stars In the Morning Sky* (Belgrade Theatre), *A Few Man Fridays* (Riverside Studios), *The Diary Of Anne Frank* (York Theatre Royal and Tour), *Nora* (Belgrade Theatre), *Cinderella* (Tobacco Factory), *Treasure Island* (Bristol Old Vic), *Nicked* (HighTide Festival 2011), *Crawling In The Dark* (Almeida), *Yerma* (WYP), *Chinglish* (UK casting Goodman Theatre Chicago & Broadway), *Too Much Pressure* (Belgrade Theatre), *One Night In November* (Belgrade Theatre, HighTide Festival 2010), *The Door Never Closes* (Almeida Theatre), *Marine Parade*, By Simon Stevens (Brighton Festival 2010).

Television & Film: *Hustle*, series 8 BBC, *Broken (Kids casting with Maggie Lunn –* Feature Film), *The Heart Fails Without Warning by Hilary Mantel* (Short film), *Trading Licks* (Short Film), *Hustle*, series 7 (for BBC), *Eliminate: Archie Cookson* (Feature Film), *Scooterman* (Short Film).

SILKI D MORRISON (STAGE MANAGER)

Theatre: *I Heart PB* by Joel Horwood (Directed by Michael Longhurst) Transfer to Edinburgh Festival 2012 and Soho Theatre, London. *Little Upper Downing Tour* (Little Bulb Theatre Company – Farnham Maltings), *Round the Twist* (Sir John Mills Theatre, Seckford Theatre) *Pinnochio* (Common Ground Theatre) *Dusk Rings a Bell* by Stephen Belber (HighTide Festival Theatre – Edinburgh Festival – Assembly Rooms and Watford Palace) *Midnight Your Time* by Adam Brace – Diana Quick (HighTide Festival Theatre – The Cut Theatre/Edinburgh Festival-Assembly Rooms 2011) *Twelfth Night* (Theatre in the Woods - Red Rose Chain), *Kabaddi, Kabaddi, Kabaddi* by Satinder Chohan (Pursued by a Bear Productions - Farnham Maltings/Kali Theatre) *Incoming* by Andrew Motion (HighTide Festival Theatre – The Cut Theatre/Latitude Festival 2011)), *Bentwater Roads* By Tony Ramsey (Eastern Angles, The Hush House) *Mansfield Park and Ride* (Eastern Angles, The Seckford Theatre)*Lincoln Road* (2009/10) by Danusia Iwaszko, *Our Nobby* (Eastern Angles, Sir John Mills Theatre/touring) *The Marvellous and Unlikely Fete of Little Upper Downing* (Little Bulb Theatre -Farnham Maltings/touring) *15 Minutes to Go, (Ex)citings* (Latitude and Greenman festival 09/10) The Hostage, Idun's Apples (New Angles Theatre) Jack and the Beanstalk (The New Wolsey Theatre) Midsummer Nights Dream (MU)

Events: Stage Manager Big Top/Main Stage – Bestival, Latitude, Playfest, Green Man Festivals

Television and Film: BBC documentaries and commercials for ITV (Producer, Bruizer Productions) music promos for *The Stereophonics, Kula Shaker, Soulsavers*(Collision Films) *McFly-The Heart Never Lies* (Pixelloft productions) Vodafone commercials (Aardman Animations) production manager on short films for Screen East and production co-ordinator on British feature film *The Rapture*.

Silki graduated with a BA Hons degree in English Literature and Drama, Middlesex University, London.

CAROLINE STEELE (ASSISTANT STAGE MANAGER)
As Assistant Stage Manager: Romeo and Juliet (Headlong, UK Tour), A British Subject (The Arts Theatre, West End), South Downs/ The Browning Version (Chichester Festival Theatre), Cloud Dance Festival (The Pleasance Theatre, Islington), Twelfth Night (Cottesloe Theatre, The National Theatre), A Month in the Country (Chichester Festival Theatre), Enron (The Noel Coward Theatre, The Royal Court Theatre and Chichester Festival Theatre) and Cyrano de Bergerac (Chichester Festival Theatre).

 HighTide Festival Theatre

New Theatre For Adventurous Audiences

'Sharp, irreverent and fresh.' Daily Telegraph

HighTide Festival Theatre is a national theatre company and engine room for the discovery, development and production of exceptional new playwrights.

Under Artistic Director Steven Atkinson, the annual HighTide Festival in Suffolk has become one of the UK's leading theatre events, and in 2012 we are excited to premiere 18 new works. HighTide's productions then transfer nationally and internationally in partnerships that have included: the Bush Theatre (2008 & 2009), National Theatre (2009), Old Vic Theatre (2010), Ambassador Theatre Group / West End (2011), to the Edinburgh Festival (2008, 2010 & 2011) and internationally to the Australian National Play Festival (2010).

HighTide receives, considers and produces new plays from all around the world, every play is read and the festival is an eclectic mix of theatre across several venues in Halesworth, Suffolk. Our artistic team and Literary Department are proud to develop all the work we produce and we offer bespoke development opportunities for playwrights throughout the year.

HighTide Festival Theatre is a National Portfolio Organisation of Arts Council England.

A Brief History

The Sixth HighTide Festival in 2012

Luke Barnes, Jon Barton, Ollie Birch, Mike Daisey, Joe Douglas, Vickie Donoghue, Tom Eccleshare, Kenny Emson, Berri George, Karis Halsall, Nancy Harris, Ella Hickson, Branden Jacobs-Jenkins, Mona Mansour, Laura Marks, Ian McHugh, Jon McLeod, Shiona Morton Laura Poliakoff, Mahlon Prince, Stella Fawn Ragsdale, Stephanie Street, Philip Wells, Nicola Werenowska, Alexandra Wood

The sixth HighTide Festival in 2012 will premiere eighteen plays in world and European premiere productions in partnerships with emerging companies and leading theatres including: Bad Physics, curious directive, Escalator East to Edinburgh, Headlong, Halesworth Middle School, Latitude Festival, Lucy Jackson, macrobert, nabokov, The Nuffield Southampton, The Public Theater, Soho Theatre, Utter.

Ella Hickson's *Boys* will transfer to The Nuffield Theatre, Southampton and Soho Theatre in a co-production with the Nuffield Theatre, Southampton and Headlong.

Luke Barnes' *Eisteddfod* will transfer to the 2012 Latitude Festival.

Joe Douglas' *Educating Ronnie* will transfer to the 2012 Edinburgh Festival produced in association with macrobert and Utter.

Luke Barnes' *Bottleneck* will premiere at the 2012 Edinburgh Festival.

Charitable Support
HighTide is a registered charity (6326484) and we are grateful to the many organisations and individuals who support our work, including Arts Council England and Suffolk County Council.

Trusts and Foundations
The Bulldog Arts Fund, The Chivers Charitable Trust, The Coutts Charitable Trust, The DC Horn Foundation, The Eranda Foundation, The Ernest Cook Charitable Trust, Esmée Fairbairn Foundation, The Foyle Foundation, The Garrick Charitable Trust, The Genesis Foundation, IdeasTap, Jerwood Charitable Foundation, The Leche Trust, The Mackintosh Foundation, The Peggy Ramsay Foundation, Scarfe Charitable Trust, The Suffolk Foundation, SOLT/Stage One Bursary for New Producers, Harold Hyam Wingate Foundation, subsidised rehearsal space provided by Jerwood Space.

Business Sponsorship
ACTIV, AEM International, Ingenious Media Plc, Lansons Communications, Plain English.

Major Donors
Peter Fincham, Nick Giles, Bill and Stephanie Knight, Clare Parsons and Tony Langham, Tony Mackintosh and Criona Palmer, Albert Scardino, Peter Wilson MBE.

With thanks to all our Friends of the Festival

HighTide Festival Theatre, 24a St John Street, London, EC1M 4AY
HighTide Writers' Centre, The Cut, Halesworth, Suffolk, IP19 8BY

0207 566 9765
hello@hightide.org.uk
www.hightide.org.uk

Artistic

Artistic Director	**Steven Atkinson**
Literary Manager	**Rob Drummer**
Projects Producer	**Philippa Wilkinson**
Voice Associate*	**John Tucker**
Music Associate*	**Tom Mills**
Resident Assistant Directors*	**Richard Fitch, Melanie Spencer**

Management

Producer	**Francesca Clark**
Consultant Producer	**Nick Giles**
Festival General Manager	**Mark Bixter**
Company Manager	**Tom Atkins**
Marketing and Development Officer	**Cad Taylor**
General Assistant (Intern)	**Victoria Dove-Clements**
Marketing Consultant	**JHI**
Marketing Design	**N9**
Press	**Borkowski.do**
Production Photography	**William Knight**
Location Photography	**Robert le Rougetel**

Production

Head of Production	**Jae Forrester**
Technical Manager	**Max Wingate**
Head of Lighting	**Matt Prentice**

HIGHTIDE FESTIVAL PRODUCTIONS LTD

President	**Peter Fincham**
Deputy Chairman	**Criona Palmer**

Patrons	Board
Sinead Cusack	**Amy Bird**
Stephen Daldry CBE	**Peter Clayton**
Sir Richard Eyre CBE	**Sue Emmas**
Sally Greene OBE	**Emma Freud OBE**
Sir David Hare	**Jo Hutchinson**
Sir Nicholas Hytner	**Joyce Hytner OBE**
Sam Mendes CBE	**James Mackenzie-Blackman**
Juliet Stevenson CBE	**Heather Newill**
Advisory Council	**Clare Parsons**
Jack Bradley	**Tali Pelman**
Robert Fox	**Mark Rhodes**
Thelma Holt CBE	**Dallas Smith**
Mel Kenyon	
Tom Morris	
Roger Wingate	

 Supported using public funding by **ARTS COUNCIL ENGLAND** LANSONS communications  Old Possums Practical Trust www.old-possums-practical-trust.org.uk ideas tap

Clockwork

Characters

Carl, *seventies*

Mikey, *seventies*

Troll Face, *forties*

Etienne, *late teens*

Sarah/Ali, *thirties*

The action takes place in a care home in Bristol, 2065.

1

06.59.00

A shabby NHS care home. **Carl**, *a chubby man in his seventies, wheels himself across the room, on his way to the toilet. He is wearing a loose-fitting Adidas tracksuit and Adidas slippers. He suddenly notices a* **Woman with Red Hair** *at the far end of the room, her face partially concealed from him. She is surrounded by a cool, eerie light which makes her seem like she could be a figment of his imagination.* **Carl** *leans forward in his wheelchair – wide-eyed, as if he's seen a ghost.*

Carl (*quietly*)   Ali?

The **Woman with Red Hair** *doesn't even flinch.*

Carl *hears footsteps approaching, hastily wheeling himself out of the spotlight.*

A large middle-aged nurse, **Troll Face**, *enters. She is holding a clipboard with today's schedule attached to it and has a toy dog squashed under one arm.*

She blinks sleepily as she examines the schedule. She turns the dog over and switches it on. Its legs move mechanically, as if it's trying to wriggle free from her grasp. She nods – satisfied it's in working order, before switching it off.

She suddenly notices **Carl.**

Troll Face   Jesus Carl, what are you doing in here?

Carl (*half whisper*)   D'you know who that woman is?

Carl *motions to where the* **Woman with Red Hair** *was standing – but she's gone.*

Troll Face   Which woman?

Carl (*confused*)   She was there a second ago.

Troll Face   You haven't been getting much sleep lately have you?

Carl *seems disconcerted by this statement.*

Carl   She was standing right there.

Troll Face   If you say so.

Carl *frowns.*

Troll Face *glances at her wrist watch, her eyes widening in surprise.*

Troll Face   You almost made me miss the wakeup call.

She produces a remote from the pocket of her uniform and points it at the tannoy in the ceiling. Annoyingly cheerful/serene music starts to play.

Carl (*jovial*)   I hate the morning music. It makes me wish I'd died in my sleep.

Troll Face *moves behind* **Carl**'s *wheelchair, no-nonsense but jovial.*

Troll Face   Let's get you back to your room.

She starts to wheel him off stage.

As **Carl** *is wheeled off stage he can't help looking back over his shoulder at the chair the woman was sitting in.*

Blackout. The morning music morphs into a Drum and Bass track.

2

10.48.00

Carl *and* **Mikey**'s *room. The back wall is lined with drawers.*

The dance music is blaring out of the tannoy.

Carl *is slumped in his wheelchair laughing.*

Mikey *sits on a plastic chair, he is also in his seventies. He has a tall skinny frame, still a good-looking man despite his age. He watches* **Carl**, *frustrated by his reaction.*

Both men are wearing Adidas hooded jumpers and Adidas Shell Toe trainers – quite a strange and comical sight given their age.

Mikey *raises his voice above the music.*

Mikey   Can you turn that off?

Carl *doesn't seem to hear him, continuing to laugh to himself.*

Mikey (*louder*)   Turn it off.

Carl *turns the music off. There is silence apart from his laughter. Finally he speaks.*

Carl   A brain tumour!

Mikey   I have to say that wasn't quite the reaction I was expecting.

Carl   You wanted tears didn't you? Snot spraying everywhere.

Mikey   'Course not, just thought it might be a bit of a shock, that's all.

Carl (*as if playing along with a joke*)   Oh no I'm not shocked – we've all gotta go sometime.

Mikey   It's just the end of a natural cycle.

Carl   How long do they think you have?

Mikey   Around a month, maybe less.

Carl (*still acting as if* **Mikey** *is joking*)   Nightmare.

Mikey (*hopeful*)   Nah I'm cool with it – feels like the right time.

Carl   So you're off to one of them clinics tonight?

Mikey (*guilty*)   'Fraid so.

Carl (*not taking him seriously*)   Well I suppose you've gotta do what you've gotta do.

Mikey (*frustrated*)   Thanks for being so supportive . . .

Carl   Bet they can't wait to toss you into a furnace – one less mouth to feed.

Mikey   I'm not being tossed into a furnace – I'm drifting off into a peaceful sleep.

Carl   That's what they want you to think.

Mikey   I can't just sit around in this chair while the tumour turns my brain into slush. There'd be more life in one of those animatronic dolls.

Carl (*indicating the heavens*)   You know them lot up there are gonna be well pissed off.

Mikey   I'm an atheist – and so are you.

Carl   But wouldn't it be the ultimate kick in the balls if the bible bashers like Tina Roberts were right all along. I don't want to have a hot poker shoved up my arse every minute of the day.

Mikey   I'm not going to have a hot poker shoved up my arse.

Carl   You don't know that for certain do you? I'm gonna convert on my deathbed just in case.

Mikey   If anyone should be kept out of heaven . . .

Carl   Oi I would be a valuable asset. Every crew needs a fat guy.

Mikey   To point and laugh at?

Carl   You'll be sorry when I'm making a cute blonde angel cream herself while you've got Hitler's dick in your mouth.

Mikey   All I'm doing is taking up space – there are thousands of people desperate for my bed.

Carl (*snorts*)   They need their heads checked.

Mikey   Better than starving to death in a skanky bedsit 'cos you can't afford a live-in carer.

Carl   Well that's their own fault isn't it – they should have thought ahead and saved up.

Mikey   What like you did you mean? You only got a place in here 'cos you lived around the corner.

Carl (*shrugs*)   So what if I did?

Mikey   I'm just saying we're the lucky ones – there are people our age who have to steal to feed themselves. Troll Face told me crimes committed by pensioners have tripled in the last decade.

Carl *snorts with laughter.*

Mikey   What's funny about that?

Carl   I was just imagining a violent gang of pensioners terrorising the streets on their mobility scooters.

Mikey   I've had more than my fair share of fun. Loved all the people I'm gonna love . . . It's time to pass the wheelchair on.

Carl (*sarcastic*)   Wow, you're a fucking legend. I wish I could be as selfless as you.

Mikey *doesn't rise to the bait. He takes a packet of cigarettes out of his pocket – there are only two left. He puts one casually in his mouth, knowing full well what reaction he'll get from* **Carl***.*

Mikey   Suppose it doesn't matter how many of these I smoke now.

Carl *swings around excitedly.*

Carl (*impish delight*)   Where d'you get those?!

Mikey (*proudly*)   Borrowed them from Troll Face while her back was turned.

Carl (*impressed*)   Finally took my advice and tried your hand at a bit of thievery. You've always been such a girl about it.

Mikey   Gotta try everything once.

Carl   My words exactly.

Mikey (*eyes* **Carl***'s excited face*)   You wouldn't want one would you?

Carl (*jovial*)   Don't fuckin' mess with me. Give one 'ere.

Mikey *grins, chucking a cigarette into* **Carl***'s lap.* **Carl** *fails to disguise his joy as he places it between his lips.*

Carl   Nicking stuff feels awesome doesn't it?

Mikey   Like coming up on pills, I wish I'd tried it sooner.

Mikey *takes out a lighter from his pocket and lights his cigarette.*
Carl *watches him in anticipation.*

Mikey *throws the lighter to* **Carl** *– it flies past him onto the floor.*

Carl   No!

Carl *skids up to the lighter in his wheelchair. He attempts to bend down towards the lighter but can't manage very far before doubling up in pain. He takes a deep breath and goes back for another go. This time he gets nearer but he still can't quite manage it. He closes his eyes, defeated. He attempts to lift himself back up but finds he can't move.*

Carl   Shit.

Mikey   Stay calm. I'll help you up.

Mikey *attempts to shuffle his chair.*

Carl *looks forlornly at his shoes, his large figure reduced to one of a small boy.*

Carl   Well this is depressing.

The cigarette falls out of his mouth on to the floor.

Mikey   Where the hell is Troll Face?

Carl (*defensive*)   I don't need her – I can get up by myself.

Mikey   Nurse!

Carl   What did I just say?

Mikey   I'm sure she's on her way. You know how long it takes her to waddle down that corridor.

Carl   She's probably in the canteen eating yesterday's rice pudding out of the dustbins.

He rests his head on his knee.

Carl Ah well at least it's something different, seeing the room from this angle. Most exciting thing that's happened to me in a good few weeks.

He suddenly raises an eyebrow inquisitively, convinced he's on to something.

Carl Wait a second – it's April the first today isn't it?

Mikey I'm not taking the piss Carl. Anyway it's November.

Carl November! Fuck me. When did you move in 'ere then?

Mikey End of July. (*Concerned.*) Did you really think it was April?

Carl Oi there's no need to make me feel bad.

Mikey Suppose there's no real need to keep track of the months in here. It's only when you start forgetting what year it is that you should get really worried!

Carl *is silent for a moment, wracking his brain.*

Mikey You do know what year it is don't you?

Carl (*worried laugh*) 'Course I do!

Mikey *waits for him to elaborate.*

Carl It's 2020.

Mikey *looks at him in stunned silence.*

Carl *laughs.*

Carl Look at your face! How fucking mentally ill d'you think I am?

Mikey I don't think I should answer that question . . . You've actually got no idea have you?

Carl (*jovial*) Fuck you – it's 2064. Thought you'd have a little more faith in me.

Mikey It's 2065.

Carl   Whatever – I was close enough.

Carl *tries to lift himself up again but he only manages a little way before stiffening in pain. He is now stuck in an awkward position – half bent over, half upright, his body contorted slightly towards* **Mikey**. *He tries to suppress an injured groan.*

Mikey (*with a smile*)   Don't move you're making it worse. (*With a smile.*) Nurse!

Carl (*through clenched teeth*)   I'm fine.

Mikey *tries to shuffle his chair again.*

Mikey   Sorry, I'm a useless roommate.

Carl   At least you're better than Psycho Harry – if Sarah hadn't moved you in here I'd still be sharing with him.

Mikey (*shudders*)   Psycho Harry. I can't believe you ended up in the same home.

Carl (*shaking his head in disbelief*)   What are the chances?

Mikey   Thank fuck they transferred him before I arrived. D'you remember that time he made you eat his /

Carl (*hastily*)   Yeah thanks for bringing up the most traumatic experience of my life. (*Grins mischievously.*) At least he got what was coming to him.

Mikey   What was that?

Carl   I swear I told you.

Mikey   Told me what?

Carl   I must have done, it's my favourite story.

Mikey   Well tell me again and then I'll know if you've already told me.

Carl (*building it up as if it's the most exciting story* **Mikey** *will ever hear*)   OK . . . wait for it, it's fucking great . . .

Mikey *waits with a mixture of excitement and frustration.*

Carl   He doesn't have any arms!

Mikey   No!

Carl   Yes!

Mikey   Actually I do think you've told me that before.

Carl (*grinning*)   He fell down the lift shaft – forgot it was broken and skidded up to it in his wheelchair. Boom! I heard it from here.

Mikey (*biting his lip to try and stop himself laughing*)   I shouldn't find that funny should I?

Carl   No it was hilarious. The best part was watching him try to feed himself when he got back from hospital. I used to yell across the canteen: 'You alright Harry, need a hand?!'

Mikey (*smirking*)   You're going straight to hell.

Carl   They've finally got the funding to make him a new pair haven't they. Boy did he bang on about it. I said: 'Listen mate, they're only arms – everyone's got 'em apart from you.'

Mikey   He always had to make a big deal out of everything.

Carl   Sarah could have just fucked off and left me with him, but she knew I'd rather have you as a roommate. I'm lucky I have a daughter who gives a shit.

Mikey *glances at his shoes.*

Mikey   You spoken to her recently?

Carl   I think so . . . (*Momentarily confused.*) All the days merge into one don't they?

Mikey (*can't help testing*)   Where did you say she worked?

Carl   San Francisco.

Mikey   Yeah but what does she actually do?

Carl *frowns, desperately trying to remember.*

Carl   She works at a . . . somewhere really impressive. (*Frustrated.*) I was dead proud when she got the job . . .

Mikey (*pretending he didn't know all along*)   She doesn't work for a law firm does she?

Carl (*relieved*)   That's it! One of the top firms in the US . . . (*Slightly concerned.*) Can't believe I forgot.

Mikey (*suddenly guilty*)   We all have off days . . .

Carl *lowers himself back down so his cheek is resting on his knee again. Strangely he seems more comfortable in this position.*

Carl   It's actually quite relaxing down here. I can see all the piss stains on the carpet.

Mikey *shuffles restlessly in his plastic chair, glancing at his wrist watch.*

Mikey   I was due a wheelchair five minutes ago. You'd think she'd try and be on time on my last day.

Carl   Give it up Mikey. I know this brain tumour malarkey's a load of bullshit.

Mikey   Seriously Carl, I'm going to the clinic tonight.

Carl (*sarcastic*)   But don't you want a birthday card from the King? That's worth sticking around for surely.

Mikey   Like he still sends 'em. Reaching a hundred means fuck-all these days – not when there's over half a million of you. Why would you want to live that long anyway?

Carl   I'd rather get my many happy returns from his missus – I'd show her how it's really done.

Mikey *stares at* **Carl** *bent over in his painful position.*

Mikey   'Course you would.

Carl   What you trying to say? Women love an elderly cripple, makes them feel all altruistic.

Mikey *wheels himself to one of the drawers built into the back wall. He opens it and retrieves a home-made card.*

Mikey   On the subject of cards . . .

He is about to hand the card to **Carl** *when* **Troll Face** *enters pushing a wheelchair. She is slightly out of breath and flustered, carrying the clipboard under her arm with the schedule attached to it.*

Mikey *quickly hides the card behind his back. He remembers the packet of cigarettes on his lap, stuffing them down his jumper.*

Troll Face   Sorry I'm late. Now Lisa's gone I always seem to be slightly behind schedule.

Carl (*hopeful*)   Are they going to fire you too Troll Face?

Troll Face *peers down at* **Carl** *stuck in his awkward position – she doesn't seem surprised.*

Troll Face   Lisa wasn't fired she was asked to leave. Sadly real chicken isn't the only thing to go when our funding gets cut.

She picks up the lighter and the cigarette from his feet.

Troll Face (*patronising*)   I think someone was trying to smoke weren't they?

Carl   You're a genius!

Troll Face   Don't be rude or I won't lift you up.

Carl   I'm fine down here.

Mikey   He wants you to help him up.

Carl   No I don't! I can do it myself.

Troll Face   Come here.

Troll Face *uses her large arms to slowly hoist* **Carl** *back into an upright position.* **Carl** *tries to shrug her off, but he can't help looking relieved when he's finally sitting up straight.*

Troll Face   There we go, that wasn't so hard was it? Now you know you're not allowed to smoke in the rooms – as punishment you won't be getting any pudding with your dinner.

Carl (*adolescent*)   But since the lift broke you hardly ever take us outside.

Mikey   It was my fault. I gave him the fag.

Troll Face   Nice try Mikey but you're the least rebellious person in here. And that includes the women's ward.

Mikey *frowns, disliking this label.*

Carl   But smoking's my basic human right.

Troll Face   I'm sorry Carl but rules are rules.

*She helps **Mikey** out of the plastic chair and into the wheelchair.*

Carl   When's the lift getting fixed then?

Troll Face   To be honest darlin' we don't know. We're waiting to hear back about our grant – and then if that falls through we'll need to organise a fundraiser.

Carl   For fuck's sake.

Troll Face   Mind your language young man.

*She notices the card on **Mikey**'s chair, picking it up.*

Troll Face   What's this?

Mikey (*hastily*)   Nothing. Just something I was going to give Carl later.

She opens the card, intrigued.

Mikey   As in not now.

Troll Face *peers at the card.*

Troll Face   Look at all your little drawings. This must have taken you ages.

Mikey (*embarrassed*)   No . . . not really.

Troll Face *hands the card to **Carl**. **Mikey** opens his mouth to protest but it's too late.*

Troll Face   Look what Mikey's made for you.

Carl *takes the card.*

Mikey   It's just a reminder of a few things. (*Self-conscious.*) I've lost most of my photos so I had to improvise.

Carl (*amused*)   Taking this joke a bit far aren't you? (*To* **Troll Face**.) Is it April the first today? Be honest with me.

Troll Face (*concerned*)   No Carl it's November.

Carl *studies the card, frowning.* **Mikey** *leans over, trying to point at the pictures.*

Mikey   The one in the top left is meant to be us out clubbing in Clockwork, giving it some in our Adidas Shell Toes.

Carl   I was never that fat was I?

Mikey (*moving swiftly on*)   Then that one in the corner is us at Glastonbury. Those triangles are meant to be tents, not tiny mountains.

Carl *suddenly snorts, pointing at one of the pictures.*

Carl   What on earth is going on here? We didn't ever have a bath together did we!

Mikey (*embarrassed*)   That's meant to be our boat trip around Amsterdam.

Carl (*laughing*)   Oh I see! These really are the shittest drawings I've ever seen.

Troll Face   Carl! Don't be so ungrateful.

Carl (*still laughing*)   Sorry Mikey, thank you for this fine selection of artwork.

Mikey *tries to hide his hurt feelings.*

Mikey   You know I've never been much good at arts and crafts – and now with my arthritis . . .

Troll Face *studies the schedule, trying to work out if there's somewhere else she needs to be.*

Carl *peers at the card.*

Carl   Wait a sec didn't I go to Amsterdam with Ali?

Mikey   It was a lads' holiday.

Carl   Was it? I swear we went there for our honeymoon.

Mikey (*firm*)   No, you didn't.

Carl *frowns, desperately trying to remember.*

Carl   Well where did I go on my honeymoon then?

Troll Face (*stepping in*)   Oh well maybe you've forgotten it for a reason. My honeymoon was a *disaster*. We were staying on this beach in Thailand, the most beautiful place I could have dreamed of – but I got a funny tummy so I was stuck in the bog the whole time.

Carl (*grinning*)   You went searching for paradise and got the shits instead – that must sum up your life perfectly Troll Face.

Troll Face *forces a smile, but we can tell she found* **Carl***'s comment hurtful.*

Troll Face   Thanks Carl, you always say such lovely things.

Carl*'s eyes suddenly light up.*

Carl   Japan! That's where we went. (*To* **Mikey**.) That's right isn't it? D'you remember me and Ali going to Japan?

Mikey *frowns, unsure how to respond.*

Mikey   Maybe . . . it was a long time ago.

Carl *winces, trying to disguise the pain shooting through his head.*

Troll Face (*concerned*)   You got another one of your headaches?

She takes a tub of pills out of the pocket of her uniform.

Troll Face   Why don't you stop being stubborn and just have one of these?

Carl   I know they're horse tranquillisers. (*To* **Mikey**.) She wants us to sit in the corner dribbling all day.

Troll Face   Don't be ridiculous.

Mikey   I'm sure that's not true.

Carl   Anyway I haven't had as much as a paracetamol my whole life, I'm not about to start with whatever that shit is – it'll fuck up my body.

Mikey (*with a smile*)   What about all those other drugs you used to take?

Carl   Those were recreational drugs, they're never bad for you.

Troll Face *holds out the tub for* **Carl**.

Troll Face   They'll make you feel so much better I promise.

Carl (*stubborn*)   Leave me alone.

Troll Face *puts the tub back in her pocket.*

Troll Face   Suit yourself.

Carl *turns his attention back to the card, snorting with laughter.*

Carl   Why have you drawn yourself bashing one out in Clockwork?

Mikey   I'm dancing! Don't you remember the Mikey dance?

Carl   Is that what you call it?

Mikey   You must remember. You took the piss out of it for years.

Carl *scrunches up his face, pretending to try and remember.*

Carl   I'm not sure I do you know. Why don't you demonstrate?

Mikey   I can't do it in a wheelchair can I?

Troll Face   That's a defeatist attitude.

Carl   Just do the arms – make Psycho Harry cry.

Troll Face   Who's Psycho Harry?

Mikey   He went to Uni with us.

Carl   You can't have forgotten Mr No-Arms.

Troll Face   Oh him! Poor love. I hear they're making him some new ones though.

Carl   Don't feel sorry for him! He scarred me for life. I should go to the Alzheimer's Institute and get it erased from my memory.

Troll Face (*hastily, to* **Mikey**)   Go on, show us your dance.

Mikey   There's no music.

Carl *points the remote at the tannoy – dance music blares out.*

Troll Face   Just wave your arms around a bit.

Mikey *crosses his arms, annoyed.*

Troll Face   That's a cross face if ever I saw one. (*She takes the remote from* **Carl** *and turns the music off.*) Remember you've got your party to look forward to later.

Carl (*confused*)   Party? What party?

Troll Face   Mikey's leaving party.

Carl (*rhetorical*)   But he's not *actually* going anywhere is he?

Troll Face   It won't be anything extravagant, obviously. But if you're very lucky there might be some cake – though I can't promise anything.

Mikey   Thanks Ruth, I do love cake.

Troll Face   No problem sweetheart. It's the least we could do.

Carl   There's nothing wrong with him!

Mikey (*to* **Troll Face**)   He thinks I'm playing a practical joke on him. Despite the fact he's spent most of our lives telling me I've got no sense of humour.

Carl   I've never met anyone so unfunny.

Troll Face *puts a hand on* **Carl**'s *shoulder.*

Troll Face   Look at my face darlin' – do I look like someone who enjoys joining in with practical jokes?

Carl *shakes his head, beginning to look worried.*

Troll Face *suddenly thinks to hand* **Carl** *her clipboard.*

Troll Face   It's even on the schedule – look.

She lifts up the first page of the schedule so **Carl** *can read the one underneath.*

Troll Face   And you know the schedule never lies.

Carl *stares at the page in shocked silence, before turning to* **Mikey** *in horror.*

Carl   You're actually leaving *tonight!*

Mikey (*guilty*)   I tried to tell you . . .

Carl *is hit by the full implication of this – there is a short moment before he is able to speak.*

Carl   Why didn't you tell me sooner?

Mikey (*looks at his trainers guiltily*)   I didn't know how.

Troll Face (*overly reassuring smile*)   Don't you worry Carl, I'll take good care of you.

Carl *looks thoroughly depressed.*

Troll Face *glances at her wrist watch.*

Troll Face (*to* **Carl***, moving behind his wheelchair*)   Let's get you to the TV room.

Troll Face *attempts to push* **Carl**'s *wheelchair off stage but* **Carl** *grabs the wheels, forcing her to grind to a halt.*

Carl   No.

Troll Face   You have to be in there by 11.15.

Troll Face *continues to try and push* **Carl**'s *chair but* **Carl** *keeps jamming the wheels.* **Troll Face** *manages to hide her frustration well.*

Carl   I'm not going.

Troll Face   Now don't be difficult sweetheart.

Carl   I want to stay with Mikey.

Etienne, *late teens, saunters into the room with an air of indifference. He is wearing an Adidas string bag on his back and brand-new Adidas Shell Toes.*

Troll Face   You're late.

Etienne   And?

Troll Face   You're not going to offer me an explanation?

Etienne   I was getting stoned in the McDonald's car park.

Troll Face   So you're late *and* high on drugs?

Etienne (*couldn't give a shit*)   Yep. What you gonna do about it?

Troll Face (*indicating* **Carl**)   Well you can start by helping me get this handsome gentleman to the TV room.

Etienne (*eyes* **Carl**)   Handsome! You wrong in the head?

Carl   Fuck you – you'll look like this in a few years.

Etienne (*grimacing*)   Nah if I looked like you I'd shoot myself in the face.

Etienne *moves behind* **Carl**'s *wheelchair and attempts to push him.*

Troll Face   Be nice to each other boys.

Carl *starts to sweat as he puts all his strength into jamming the wheelchair.*

Etienne *soon manages to overpower* **Carl**, *grinning triumphantly as he pushes him across the stage.* **Carl**'s *arms dangle down on either side of the chair – too exhausted to fight back.*

Etienne   You're *weak* – my little sister would have put up more of a fight.

Carl *grits his teeth to hide his humiliation.*

Mikey   Can I come with him?

Carl   Don't give in! We can defeat them if we both work together.

Troll Face *peers at her clipboard sceptically.*

Troll Face (*to* **Mikey**)   You're not scheduled to be in the TV room till your party at 4.

Mikey   This is my last day Troll Face. (*Hastily.*) I mean Ruth. Surely you can make an exception . . .

Mikey *smiles at her charmingly.*

Troll Face   Look at you in your adorable jumper. How can I say no to that?

She moves behind **Mikey**'s *wheelchair.*

Mikey *tugs at his jumper – embarrassed and patronised.*

Etienne   You lot shouldn't be allowed to wear Adidas – it's just wrong.

Carl   You're the one who shouldn't be wearing it. (*Indicating* **Etienne**'s *shoes.*) We had those trainers before you were even born.

Troll Face *starts to wheel* **Mikey** *off stage.*

Troll Face (*to* **Carl**)   We're off to have a nice time in the TV room. See you in there.

Mikey *looks back at* **Carl** *and shrugs: 'What choice do we have?'* **Troll Face** *wheels him off stage.*

Carl (*yelling after her*)   Beast!

He is left alone with **Etienne**.

Etienne   So is it time for round two or you gonna come quietly?

Carl *slumps down dejectedly in his chair – he doesn't have the energy.*

Etienne (*grins*)   That's what I thought.

He seems to take great joy in wheeling **Carl** *off stage. Blackout.*

3

11.30.00

Carl *and* **Mikey** *sit in the TV room, both in wheelchairs.* **Carl** *is wearing a virtual reality headset.*

Mikey   I'm sure it's my turn now.

Carl   No way, I've had it for like five minutes.

Mikey (*frustrated*)   Well tell me what's happening then.

Carl   Hundreds of naked women are sprinting towards me along a beach.

He pretends to duck out of the way of an imaginary object.

Carl   There are tits flying at me from all angles.

Mikey (*jovial*)   Fuck off what are you really watching?

Carl (*takes it off*)   Nothing – it's broken.

Mikey (*shaking his head in disbelief*)   Soon they're be nothing left to entertain us.

He glances at his watch.

Mikey   The party should be a laugh though.

Carl   I'm not coming to the party.

Mikey (*trying to hide his disappointment*)   Why not?

Carl *shrugs nonchalantly.*

Carl   Got other stuff on.

Mikey *frowns, realising* **Carl** *is being difficult on purpose.*

Mikey   Like what?

Carl   I already promised someone else I'd hang out with them. Can't back out now or I'll look like a right rude cunt. You know how it is.

Mikey   Why don't you bring 'em along?

Carl   Nah they won't wanna come.

Mikey   Why's that?

Carl   They told me they think you're boring.

Mikey   You've got some nice mates.

Carl   I never said they were a mate, just promised I'd hang out with them.

Mikey   But you've always loved a good party.

Carl   I do love a good party, I'll give you that. But an actual party – a piss-up, a rave, or an orgy – not a bunch of cripples eating cake.

Mikey   We don't know for certain there'll be any cake.

Carl   Well I'm definitely not coming then.

Mikey   Fine, be a total dickhead – it's only our last day together.

Carl *shakes the virtual reality headset at him.*

Carl   And whose fault is that! This wasn't the deal Mikey. The whole point of you transferring here was so we didn't have to die alone like those Japanese men who weren't found till their faces had rotted off.

Mikey (*guiltily*)   One of us was always gonna go first. You won't want to share a room with me when I'm all shrivelled and secreting fluids out of every orifice.

Carl   That's no different to how you are now.

Mikey   I want to go with dignity.

Carl   Dignity's over-rated.

Mikey *lowers his voice, nodding his head subtly towards the corner of the room.*

Mikey   Kelly keeps looking over here. I think she likes you.

Carl (*grimacing*)   Someone really needs to get rid of that rice pudding round her mouth. It's revolting.

Mikey   She was probably pretty hot back in the day.

Carl   That saggy scrotum? You could hang Christmas tree decorations from the folds of her skin.

Mikey   Shhh.

Carl   What? She's deaf.

Mikey   Is she?

Carl   I've always thought so.

Mikey (*confused*)   Maybe you're right.

Carl *suddenly notices something, smirking.*

Carl   Well there's our answer.

Mikey   What?

Carl   She's giving us the finger.

Mikey (*squints*)   Is she?

Carl   It's just rising extremely slowly. Like your dick when you see Troll Face.

Mikey (*still squinting*)   Oh yeah there it is, well spotted.

Carl *shouts across the room.*

Carl   You know where to shove that love!

Mikey   Carl! That's not the way to make friends.

Carl   I don't want to make friends! (*A little shamefaced.*) I want things to stay as they are . . .

Mikey (*guilty*)   So do I . . . but I just can't stay here any more.

Carl   Why?! It's really not that bad.

Mikey (*snorts*)   You know you whinge more than anyone else.

Carl   We're lucky – the home where they sent Psycho Harry has like twenty-five to a room. Everyone pissing and shitting on each other – it's just like the Scottish homes.

Mikey (*grinning*)   You're such a liar.

Carl   But think of all the fun we have! We listen to the radio together – for at least an hour a week. I admit most of the time it's utter shite like *The Archers* – but you always say it reminds you of your mum.

Mikey   It does remind me of my mum.

Carl   We have a cheeky fag at 2 in the morning when the old Troll's gone to bed. And what about last week when we stole that whisky out of her cupboard – that was a good night wasn't it?

Mikey (*conceding*)   Yeah that was a laugh.

Carl   And all the old times too, the ones in my card. Think how much fun it will be to sit around and reminisce for another month.

Mikey *frowns, he clearly doesn't agree.*

Mikey   I think we've done enough of that. I'd rather talk about something else – like football, or how much our balls have shrunk.

Carl   You're pissed off 'cos I brought up the honeymoon aren't you?

Mikey (*lying badly*)   No . . .

Carl   It's alright I understand, I know it's still a bit of a sore subject.

Mikey *looks increasingly uncomfortable but tries to disguise it.*

Mikey   It's not . . .

Carl   You always go all weird when she comes up in conversation. (*Leans forward in his chair.*) Come on hit me with it. If you're really leaving tonight you should get everything off your chest.

Mikey (*unconvincing*)   There's nothing to say.

Carl   You sure?

Mikey   'Course . . .

Carl *perks up.*

Carl   OK then, cool. I won't ask you again.

There is a moment's pause.

Carl   I know you still think about her though. I hear you talking to her in your sleep.

Mikey (*embarrassed*)   No I don't.

Carl   It's nothing to be ashamed of. This morning I saw a woman with red hair in the waiting room – I almost had a heart attack.

Mikey *is clearly troubled by this comment, but tries to seem casual.*

Mikey   We'll it's not like it could have been her.

Carl (*unsure*)   'Course not . . . It was probably one of those hallucinations I sometimes get. Apparently it might be the LSD working its way out of my body. You sure you're not getting them too?

Mikey (*anxious*)   I don't think so.

Carl   I guess it would be hard to tell. For all you know I could be a hallucination. You could just be sitting in the corner talking to yourself.

Mikey   Don't say that.

Carl   Troll Face could be one too – that would be kind of horrifying wouldn't it?

Mikey (*can't help smiling*)   Stop it, you're freaking me out.

He glances at his wrist watch.

Mikey   Lunchtime soon – have you seen the menu?

Carl   Chicken and mash.

Mikey   Real chicken or fake chicken?

Carl   What d'you think?

Mikey *grimaces in disgust.*

Carl   It's not that bad – it just tastes a bit fishier than real chicken. The stuff they feed them in the Totterdown home's much worse. They don't even get fake meat – just porridge oats and sawdust.

Mikey (*smiling, clearly doesn't believe him*)   Is that right?

Carl *studies* **Mikey** *for a second.*

Carl   So there's really nothing you wanna say to me?

Mikey   No! I thought you weren't going to bring that up again.

Carl   Oh yeah, sorry . . .

Carl *slumps back in his chair, he looks across at* **Mikey**, *unable to drop the subject.*

Carl   D'you remember that first time we saw her in Clockwork? It was not my finest hour.

Mikey *can't help smirking.*

Mikey   Didn't you tell her you used to have wet dreams about her in school?

Carl (*as if* **Mikey***'s got completely the wrong end of the stick*)   No . . . I told her I used to dream about her trainers. Those luminous green and yellow. It's not my fault she thought that was creepy.

Mikey (*jovial*)   The trainers, of course!

Carl   I panicked alright. It had already gone so badly. The friendly punch on the arm had been a lot harder than intended. Her drink was all down the front of her dress. It was safe to say she wasn't gonna fall for any of the smooth chat-up lines I'd prepared.

Mikey   So you told her you'd been wanking off over her shoes?

Carl   It wasn't like that.

Mikey   Wasn't it?

Carl   In the dream we'd always be running through a park together – she'd be wearing her green and yellow trainers and I'd be barefoot. And we'd run and run along this gravelly path, and my feet are getting all scratched up – bleeding everywhere. But then Ali suddenly skids to a halt and takes off one of her trainers – all steaming and moist 'cos she'd been wearing them without socks – and gently slides it on to my foot. And I could feel it so clearly, my cold foot sliding into her sweaty trainer – it was the nicest thing I'd ever felt. The kindest thing anyone's ever done for me.

Mikey (*biting his lip*)   You said that to her?

Carl   That was the gist of it yeah.

Mikey *snorts with laughter.*

Carl   It's not my fault! I've always found it hard to judge what women find offensive. Luckily I managed to salvage the situation by giving her some free weed.

Mikey   And that was the start of a beautiful friendship.

Carl   That was the problem – 'friendship'. A relationship with a female that doesn't involve fucking is of no use to anyone.

Mikey   I'm sure some people might disagree with you about that.

Carl   Ali led me to believe she wanted this fine male specimen beside her on a cold winter's night. She was always flirting with me, with those big 'fuck me as hard as you can in the fanny' eyes. But I was a bit larger back then wasn't I? Chubby some might say . . . Whereas you were the whole package weren't you?

For a second **Carl***'s eyes flash with bitterness.*

Mikey *sighs and rolls his eyes – not this again.*

Mikey   We were *teenagers*. I wasn't gonna not go out with Ali just 'cos you liked her. Only girls do lame things like that.

Carl *shrugs sulkily.*

Carl   I guess it's not your fault she was so shallow . . . Anyway she saw sense in the end.

Mikey *frowns, resenting this comment.*

Mikey   That's what happened is it?

Carl   I'm sorry but I couldn't have been expected to turn her down – my dick would have never forgiven me.

Troll Face *enters.*

Troll Face   What on earth are you two talking about?

Carl   I was just saying my dick/

Mikey (*butting in*)   We used to like the same girl at one point, that's all.

Troll Face   Aw isn't that sweet.

Carl   Don't patronise us, we've had more sex than you'll ever have. Especially Mikey – he attracted girls like a fly-catcher sprinkled with cocaine and Rohypnol.

Troll Face (*holds out her hand*)   Headset please.

Carl (*handing it over*)   It's broken.

Troll Face   Is it?

She bashes the headset against the wall, before putting it on herself.

Troll Face (*wearing headset*)   There we go – good as new.

Carl   Can I have it back then?

Troll Face (*taking off the headset*)   Sorry hun it's due in the other wing.

Carl   This is ridiculous! They used to be as common as laptops.

Troll Face   Well if there weren't so many of you lot there might be a little bit more of everything.

Carl   But my brain needs stimulating! And so does Mikey's – his has a tumour in it.

Troll Face *smiles, suddenly getting an idea.*

Troll Face   This is the perfect time to try out that activity you never want to do.

Carl's *eyes widen in alarm.*

Carl   No, anything but that.

Blackout.

4

14.50.00

Carl *and* **Mikey** *each have an easel in front of them, painting on to large pieces of white paper with brightly coloured poster paint – concentrating hard. They are back in their bedroom, both in wheelchairs.*

Carl *is painting a naked woman – as if he's in a life drawing class which happens not to have a model. The woman is unintentionally out of proportion – a huge head, large breasts, but tiny arms and legs.*

Mikey *is painting a simple but picturesque scene – a boat floating on a bright blue sea, a large sun shining down.*

Troll Face *stands in between them. She is holding a toy dog under one arm.*

Troll Face (*to* **Carl**)   See I knew you'd enjoy yourself.

Carl (*determined not to concede*)   I didn't realise I'd get to paint a naked woman did I? Thought I'd have to do something lame like Mikey's.

Mikey *doesn't look up, too engrossed in splodging yellow paint in the corner of his picture.*

Troll Face *peers down at* **Carl**'s *painting.*

Troll Face   I have to admit this isn't quite what I was expecting you to draw.

Carl   You said paint one of your happiest memories – surely my beautiful naked wife is an obvious choice.

Troll Face (*amused*)   That's what she looked like is it?

Carl   More or less . . . (*To* **Mikey**.) This is kind of what Ali looked like naked isn't it?

Mikey *forces himself to look across at* **Carl**'s *painting, frowning with disapproval.*

Mikey (*annoyed*)   No, it's not.

Carl   'Suppose you weren't with her when she looked like this. You got her from sixteen to eighteen – lucky bastard.

Mikey (*irritated*)   Can we change the subject?

Carl (*to* **Troll Face**, *loud whisper*)   He doesn't like being reminded we fucked the same woman – he can be a bit old-fashioned sometimes.

Troll Face *notices* **Mikey** *is glaring at his painting, red-faced – it's definitely time to change the subject. She hands* **Carl** *the dog under her arm.*

Troll Face   This is for you.

Carl *puts down his paint brush and takes the dog from her hands. He holds it out in front of him with an air of suspicion.*

Troll Face   I know you're a bit down about Mikey leaving, but these animatronic pets are really good at helping residents deal with loneliness and depression.

Carl *slowly looks from the dog, to* **Mikey**, *and then back to* **Troll Face** – *clearly very unimpressed.*

Troll Face   Give it a stroke under its chin – it'll rub its head against your hand. Very lifelike. (*Enticing.*) If you show the dog love it'll love you right back.

Carl *thrusts the dog's friendly face up towards* **Troll Face**.

Carl   Look at that face – he doesn't give a fuck about me. It's a machine – a computer programme *pretending* to love me.

Troll Face   Well if you have to put it like that.

Carl   I remember the first time I saw one of these – it was on the news at my gran's house. An old people's home in Japan had given its residents this robotic *seal* to see if it stopped them wanting to throw themselves out the nearest window. I can still see it now – the image of this tiny wrinkly Japanese man, abandoned by his family and close to death, cradling this ridiculous white fluffy seal in his arms like a baby. It was single-handedly the most depressing thing I'd ever seen. (*Pointing the dog at* **Mikey**.) And now here we are being palmed off with this piece of crap. The exact same model they gave my mum when they forced her to put Winston down.

Troll Face   What did your mum think of her robotic dog? Didn't she find it comforting?

Carl *frowns, caught out.*

Carl   By then she didn't know what was going on. She even insisted on having the grotty thing buried with her.

Troll Face   So she loved it?

Carl   She thought it was real.

Troll Face   Exactly – that's how advanced the technology was, even back then.

Mikey   My uncle had an animatronic cat he was very close to.

Carl   Who the fuck cares!

Mikey *looks momentarily offended.*

Carl   It's just slightly depressing to think that after you leave I'm gonna be stuck with this *thing* as my only source of companionship.

Troll Face   Just try giving it a stroke.

Carl   You'll be replaced soon Troll Face – they're gonna build an army of new healthcare workers out of metal and prosthetics. They'll be able to wash ten shitty arses in the time it takes you to wash one.

Troll Face (*amused*)   Is that so?

Carl   Unless they decide it will be cheaper to just upgrade you Troll Face. Replace some of your limbs with aluminium and upload extra memory into your brain so you can remember all the residents' names.

Troll Face   I don't think you realise how lucky you are to have that dog at all. They're not as common as they used to be.

Carl   Oh I'm lucky am I? If I have to rely on a robot for love I at least want it to be one of those hot animatronic women. I know there are homes that still have them. 'Course they can't do everything a real female can do . . . but they can hold you as you cry yourself to sleep. Hug you without pulling away.

Troll Face   Carl sweetheart you know we can barely afford to feed you decent food, let alone order you an animatronic woman to hold you while you sleep. Only the private homes could do a thing like that.

Carl   I suppose it did get a bit creepy – pensioners with enough cash requesting *exactly* what they wanted.

Troll Face   Give the dog a chance Carl.

Carl *starts to squeeze the dog violently in his hands, as if he's trying to break off its legs.*

Carl   This is nothing like a real dog. A real dog would be dead by now, or at least wheezing.

Troll Face *attempts to release his grip.*

Troll Face   Now love there's no need for that. I know it's old but it's still an expensive piece of equipment.

Troll Face *manages to prise the dog free. She hands it to* **Mikey**.

Mikey *strokes the dog under its chin. His face breaks into a surprised smile.*

Mikey   It is actually pretty realistic.

Troll Face   See Carl, Mikey has the right attitude.

Carl   Mikey's an idiot.

Mikey (*hurt*)   Cheers.

Etienne *casually strolls into the room.*

Troll Face   That was a long lunch break.

Etienne (*couldn't give a shit*)   Yep.

Troll Face *pulls him up a plastic chair.*

Etienne *slumps down in the chair, legs spread wide.*

Troll Face   I hope you remembered to bring a book to read them.

Etienne (*mock offence*)   What d'you take me for?

He retrieves a book from his string bag. He reads the title as if he's never heard of it before.

Etienne   'Harry Potter'.

Carl *and* **Mikey** *groan.*

Carl   Why? (*Looking towards the heavens, louder.*) Why!

Etienne   My teacher said it's a classic. You lot are meant to love classics.

Mikey   Someone *always* brings in 'Harry Potter'.

Carl   It's a *children's* book. We're not children!

A phone can be heard ringing down the corridor. **Troll Face** *moves off stage.*

Troll Face (*to* **Etienne**)   Behave.

She notices **Carl** *is eagerly waiting for her to leave. She frowns, suspicious.*

Troll Face   You too . . .

She leaves the three of them alone.

Carl (*to* **Mikey**)   Give me the dog.

Mikey (*sceptical*)   What for?

Carl   Just hand it over.

Mikey *hands him the dog.* **Carl** *immediately chucks the dog as hard as he can over the other side of the room. It hits the back wall with a loud clang.* **Mikey** *shakes his head in disapproval.*

Etienne *indicates* **Carl**'*s painting.*

Etienne   What the fuck is that?

Carl   A naked woman. Haven't you ever seen one before?

Etienne (*boyish and defensive*)   Yeah, 'course I have . . .

He flicks through the book.

Etienne   So you don't want me to read this to you then?

Carl/Mikey   No.

Etienne *grins mischievously, finding a page in the middle of the book and starting to read out loud.*

Carl *and* **Mikey** *cover their ears and start humming loudly, drowning him out.*

Etienne *stops reading, watching them with a mixture of contempt and amusement.*

Carl *and* **Mikey** *soon realise he's stopped, taking their hands away from their ears sheepishly.*

Mikey   That may have seemed slightly childish, but you left us no choice.

Etienne *puts the book back in his bag.*

Etienne   Didn't want to read it anyway.

Carl   Why don't you piss off then?

Etienne   You think I wanna be stuck here with you losers? This bullshit's just part of my probation.

Mikey   You're a criminal? (*To* **Carl**.) Troll Face left us alone with a criminal?

Carl   Look at him he's just a baby. Kelly's more intimidating.

Etienne *leans forward in his chair, confrontational.*

Etienne   Is that right?

He takes a stanley knife out of his pocket.

Mikey *is taken aback but* **Carl** *doesn't seem fazed.*

Mikey (*hastily*)   He was only joking. We find you very intimidating.

Etienne   D'you want to know why I was arrested?

Carl (*completely uninterested*)   No.

Etienne   Me and my mate Joel used to rob pensioners as they walked home at night. It's pretty funny I've ended up 'ere isn't it?

Mikey   I can't say I find that particularly funny . . .

Etienne   We cut one up too.

Carl *suddenly yawns incredibly loudly.* **Etienne** *looks at him in absolute shock.* **Carl** *retrieves a porn magazine from his drawer and starts to flick through it absentmindedly. He yawns again, glancing at his wrist watch.*

Etienne Yeah try and pretend you're not shitting yourself. But you better start showing me some respect – I'm a dangerous man.

Carl (*fake coughs*) Bullshit.

Mikey Carl!

Etienne *jumps up from his chair, knife in hand.*

Etienne What did you just say?

Mikey He didn't say anything. He's an old man – he coughs all the time.

Carl I said you're talking out of your arse. Trying to hide the fact your dick's the size of a . . .

He momentarily can't think of an insult.

Carl (*aware it's a crap insult*) Sausage roll . . .

Etienne *frowns, unsure whether to be offended.*

Etienne What one of them big long ones you get in 'Greg's' – or those tiny ones you get at kids' parties?

Carl *and* **Mikey** *speak at the same time.*

Mikey (*hastily*) A big long one. **Carl** A *tiny* sausage roll.

Etienne (*to* **Carl**) You're gonna pay for that.

He advances towards **Carl**.

Carl *doesn't look up from the magazine. He turns the page very loudly.* **Etienne** *is suddenly distracted by the naked images.*

Etienne Are those real women?

Carl *nods.*

Etienne Without underwear?

Carl *nods again, still not looking up.*

Etienne *becomes genuinely excited.*

Etienne Fuck me you've got proper old-school porn! You can't get that *anywhere*.

Carl   Censorship gone mad. I predicted it would happen.

Mikey   I wish we could have gone to the demonstration.

Carl   It's a basic human right.

Etienne   Like smoking.

Carl   Exactly.

Etienne (*tentative*)   Could I maybe . . . have a look?

Carl *finally looks up at him, sizing him up.*

Carl   What can you give me in return?

Etienne   Man, don't be cruel.

Carl   Come on boy, these are hard times.

Etienne   What sort of thing you after?

Carl/Mikey   Fags.

Mikey   And a lighter.

Etienne *begrudgingly takes a packet of cigarettes out of his pocket and offers them both one.* **Carl** *takes two.* **Mikey** *copies him.* **Etienne** *shakes his head as he hands* **Carl** *a lighter.*

Etienne   What you gotta clean me out for?

Carl *hands* **Etienne** *the magazine.*

Carl   Life's unfair. You should know – you used to rob pensioners.

Etienne *puts the knife back in his pocket and sits down on his chair, eagerly flicking through the pages.* **Carl** *lights his cigarette then hands the lighter to* **Mikey**. *They both breathe in the nicotine gleefully.*

Etienne *is also enjoying himself immensely.*

Etienne   I take back what I said – this is definitely worth four fags and a lighter.

Mikey   Troll Face is going to be furious.

Carl   I hope so. I love the way her jowls tremble when she gets mad.

Etienne   D'you know what I found the other day – robot porn.

Carl (*highly amused*)   Amazing.

Mikey   That was always gonna happen.

Etienne   It's the way people are getting round the ban – there's no law against robots showing their tits. Some of them look well realistic. But no doubt that'll be off the shelves soon too.

Carl   I'm actually feeling sorry for you. (*To* **Mikey**.) Imagine growing up without porn.

Mikey *shakes his head solemnly.*

Mikey   It doesn't bear thinking about.

Etienne   I thought it was just my granddad who was a perv, but you lot are all the same.

Carl   Surely everyone's a pervert?

Etienne   Yeah but Granddad takes it to another level. When he started forgetting things he went to the Alzheimer's Institute to get one of them memory chips put in – and while he was there he thought he'd upload all his favourite porn right into his brain to make sure he never lost it. There was shit loads, I doubt there was any room left in his head for my gran.

Carl   They must be making a mint charging people for that sort of thing.

Etienne   They'll do whatever you want for a price. I think it's disgusting – Granddad shouldn't be allowed to cram his brain full of filth.

Mikey (*indicating the magazine* **Etienne***'s reading*)   You're telling me you wouldn't given half the chance?

Etienne   That's different.

Mikey   Why?

Etienne   I'm seventeen. You lot aren't still meant to be . . .

Carl/Mikey   Horny.

Etienne (*puts his hands over his ears in disgust*)   Man, don't say it!

Carl   Why not? We've got the same body parts – what else are we gonna to do with it?

Etienne (*grimaces*)   I'm gonna be sick.

Footsteps are heard approaching.

Carl *quickly flicks his cigarette under* **Etienne**'s *chair.* **Mikey** *copies him.* **Etienne** *is too engrossed in the magazine to notice. As* **Troll Face** *enters he instinctively hides the magazine behind his back.*

Troll Face   Who's been smoking?

Carl *subtly points under* **Etienne**'s *chair.*

Troll Face (*to* **Etienne**)   Oh you've really pushed it this time!

Etienne   What the fuck! They were the ones smoking.

Carl   He used to mug pensioners in the street.

Troll Face (*outraged*)   Is that true?

Etienne   No! I was lying about that shit.

Carl *grins, gaining immense satisfaction from watching* **Etienne** *squirm.*

Troll Face   Right you're going to have to spend an extra hour in the women's ward to make up for this.

Etienne   But /

Troll Face   No arguing or I won't sign your form.

Etienne *glares at* **Carl** *and* **Mikey**. *They try hard to stop themselves grinning.*

Troll Face   And don't think I didn't see what you were reading. I'm not blind you know.

Etienne   Bet your husband is though!

Troll Face *crosses her arms, annoyed.*

Troll Face   You're on thin ice.

Carl (*impressed*)   He's only been here ten minutes and it's like he's one of us.

Etienne *is clearly disturbed by this thought. He quickly rises from his chair.*

Etienne   Right then, women's ward is it?

He tries to make his exit with the magazine concealed under his arm.

Carl   Oi.

Etienne *turns round, his face expressing fake ignorance.*

Etienne   What?

Carl *holds out his hand for the magazine.*

Carl   You didn't think I'd let you steal my most valuable possession did you?

Etienne *looks like he's about to give it back – but suddenly rips out one of the pages, chucking the rest of the magazine on the floor. He bounces out of the room, brandishing the precious page in his hand.*

Etienne   Go fuck yourself cripple.

He exits.

Carl   What a charming young man.

Troll Face *yells after him.*

Troll Face   That's an extra two hours you've earned yourself there.

She picks up the toy dog from the floor.

Troll Face   What's this doing down here?

Carl *shrugs innocently.*

Troll Face *frowns, putting the dog down on the plastic chair.*

She checks her wrist watch.

Troll Face (*to* **Mikey**)   We better get all your things packed before the party.

She opens **Mikey**'s *drawer and retrieves a rucksack, starting to fill it with the objects inside the drawer.*

Carl *watches her start to remove his friend's life from the room.*

Carl (*panicking*)   Put those back. It's still early – he might change his mind.

Mikey (*guilty*)   Carl I've made my decision.

Carl (*stressed*)   But what about me?

Troll Face   Everything's going to be fine.

Carl (*to* **Mikey**)   You don't care if I'm left by myself – I *knew* you were still pissed off I stole her off you!

Carl *feels the onset of another excruciating headache.*

Carl   Fuck.

Troll Face *takes a tub of pills out of her pocket.*

Troll Face   Come on now love, have one of these.

Mikey   If you're in pain why don't you just take one?

Troll Face *takes a pill out of the tub.*

Troll Face   Open wide.

Carl *clamps his mouth shut.*

Troll Face (*bending over him*)   This isn't some sort of conspiracy Carl – I'm just trying to help you.

Carl *leans away from her, determined not to let her win.*

Carl   You're gonna have to force it down me.

Troll Face *rolls her eyes, putting the pill back in the tub.*

Troll Face (*disheartened*)   Well it can't be said I didn't try. (*To* **Mikey**.) I have to go and set up your party. I'll be back to help you with your packing in a bit.

She exits.

Mikey *picks up the rucksack* **Troll Face** *left by his drawer, continuing to pack objects into it.*

Carl *frowns as he watches* **Mikey**.

Carl   I can't believe you're going to leave me here with that cruel witch.

Mikey   Let's not argue. I want us to have fun at the party.

Carl   Fun!

Mikey   It's our last night out together.

Carl   It's gonna be the most depressing experience imaginable.

His face suddenly lights up.

Carl   Hold on.

He wheels himself over to his drawer.

Mikey (*dubious*)   What?

Carl   I just need to check something.

Mikey *reluctantly moves aside.* **Carl** *opens the top drawer, rummaging around. Finally he produces a battered boiled sweet tin. He has some trouble opening the stiff lid. He grins when he sees what's inside, turning to* **Mikey** *excitedly.*

Carl   I'd forgotten all about them.

Mikey (*wary*)   I'm guessing they're not sweets.

Carl *chucks* **Mikey** *the tin.* **Mikey** *frowns when he sees what it contains.*

Mikey   I hope that's not what I think it is.

Carl   'Course it is!

Mikey (*shocked*)   What you still got them for? They must be over forty years old.

Carl   A special occasion – like a party!

Mikey (*shaking his head adamantly*)   No way. Definitely not.

Carl   But this is perfect! You just said you wanted us to have fun.

Mikey   Not that kind of fun. What if our bodies can't handle it any more – it could kill us!

Carl   Well it's not like that matters to you. And to be honest I can't think of a better way to go.

Mikey   What's the point? It's not like we can jump up and dance – it'll be depressing.

Carl   Like I said earlier, all you need is your arms to throw out some good moves.

Mikey   I think it's a very, very bad idea. (*Firm.*) I'm not doing it.

Fade to black. 'The Archers' *theme tune blares out of the darkness.*

When the lights come up again both men are instinctively bobbing their heads to the music, wide-eyed.

Mikey (*excited*)   I've never noticed how sick this tune was before.

Carl   I know!

'The Archers' *theme tune comes to an end and the show starts.* **Carl** *immediately turns the hi-fi off.*

Carl   That's enough of that.

Mikey (*disappointed*)   I wish the music didn't have to end.

Carl   I feel amazing – my nipples are tingling.

Mikey   It does feel pretty good.

Carl (*satisfied*)   Not such a bad idea after all.

Mikey (*happily*)   Guess not – and we're both still alive!

Carl   If you don't leave we can sit around and do this all the time – there's still like fifteen left.

Mikey *seems to be considering this for a second, but then shakes his head.*

Mikey   No Carl, I really do have to go. (*He catches sight of his rucksack.*) Shit I have to pack. I haven't packed!

Mikey *continues to clear the few remaining objects from inside his drawer and stuff them into his rucksack. It only takes him a couple of seconds to pack everything.*

Mikey   That didn't take as long as I thought it would.

Carl *wheels himself over to his drawer.*

Carl   Right let's get ourselves ready for this party.

He opens the drawer and retrieves an old pot of hair gel. He rubs a small amount in between his fingers and then runs them through his hair.

Carl   Come 'ere.

Mikey *leans his head towards him.* **Carl** *takes a huge lump of gel out of the pot and smears it on to* **Mikey**'s *hair, slicking it back.* **Carl** *leans back and admires his handiwork.*

Mikey   How do I look?

Mikey *looks comically sleazy with his greasy hair and Adidas jumper.*

Carl   Fuckable.

Mikey's *face lights up; he touches his slimy hair.*

Mikey   Nice.

Carl   Now all we need is some music.

Carl *points the remote at the tannoy. A Drum and Bass starts to play.*

Carl   D'you remember when they used to play this in Clockwork – we'd go mental.

Mikey   'Course I do.

They enjoy the music for a short moment.

5

16.30.00

Carl and **Mikey** *are sitting side by side in their wheelchairs in the corner of the TV room. An empty plastic chair has been left beside them.*

Mikey (*loud whisper*)   D'you think Troll Face can tell we're high?

Carl   I hope so. Your squeaky-clean image will be ruined.

They look across the room as if they're people-watching.

Carl   It's a bit of a poor turnout isn't it? People must hate you more than I thought.

Mikey (*trying to hide his hurt feelings*)   Oi I've only been here a couple of months . . . And it hasn't been easy to make friends with you hanging around – you scare people off.

Carl   No I don't! I'm a very popular guy.

Mikey   Everyone apart from Kelly – I don't know what she sees in you.

Carl   She knows I have a massive cock.

Mikey   Where would she have got that bullshit idea from?

Carl   'Cos it's a fact! You know how girls love to gossip.

Mikey (*snorts*)   Yeah 'cos you've had sex with a female while you've been in here.

Carl   I have! With *loads* of them, embarrassingly – but what else am I meant to do to pass the time?

Mikey   Where is Kelly anyway? I thought at least she'd turn up.

Carl (*grinning*)   You fancy her don't you?

Mikey (*grimacing*)   No I don't!

Carl (*points a finger at him knowingly*)   Ah so she's good enough for me but not for you eh?

Mikey   I never said that, I just meant . . .

Carl   I'm listening.

Mikey   Michelle's more my type.

Carl   Good choice, tits haven't quite reached the knees.

Mikey   She doesn't seem as angry and bitter as all the others. Sometimes I think I can see a glimmer of hope left in her eyes.

Etienne *approaches them holding a plate of biscuits and a jug of water – a pile of plastic party cups squashed under his arm. He has trouble putting the jug and cups down on the floor.* **Carl** *and* **Mikey** *snigger as they watch his efforts.*

Etienne   D'you want a cheap shitty biscuit that tastes like cardboard?

Mikey   Isn't there any cake?

Etienne   Nah that plan fell through.

Mikey (*genuinely disappointed*)   Oh, I was really looking forward to some cake.

Etienne   This is all you're gonna get.

Carl (*grabbing a biscuit*)   I'll have one.

He stuffs the biscuit eagerly into his mouth – but starts to grimace as he chews.

Mikey *reaches out for a biscuit but then retracts his hand.*

Mikey   Actually my stomach's the size of a walnut.

Carl (*while chewing*)   This is the shittest party I've ever been to.

Etienne *snorts as he sits down on the plastic chair, putting the biscuits down on the floor.*

Etienne   Like you've ever been to a good party. I bet you used to sit around a fire and read books to each other and shit.

Mikey (*mock offence*)   How old d'you think we are?

Carl *turns to* **Etienne**, *as if he's about to give him life-changing advice.*

Carl   You should party as hard as you can while you still have the chance.

Etienne   I think I can manage that.

Carl   I'm being serious. 'Cos one day you'll be trapped in a room with an equally shitty carpet. (*Indicating the offstage party guests.*) This will be your social life in a couple of years.

Etienne (*snorts*)   Yeah right.

He can't help slowly glancing across the room – a look of terror forming on his face.

Etienne   I'll have kids though. They'll look after me.

Carl   Ah but will they? My daughter moved to San Francisco. Or you might end up not having kids after all, like Mikey.

Mikey *bites his tongue.*

Etienne   Why d'you not have kids – you couldn't get a girl to commit?

Mikey (*annoyed*)   That's not what happened.

Etienne   Oh I see – you were a player.

Carl   He kinda was.

Mikey   That's bollocks.

Etienne   And now you're shacked up with him instead – that's gotta hurt.

Carl   Fuck off.

Etienne   I just feel sorry for him, that's all.

Mikey   I don't need your pity.

Etienne   Seriously, it must be shit not having a family.

Mikey (*annoyed*)   I have someone in my life who cares about me very much, but that's none of your business.

Carl (*confused*)   Who's that?

Mikey (*hastily*)   No one you know.

Carl (*jealous*)   If they care about you so much why'd they never come and visit?

Mikey *stumbles over his words, regretting bringing this up.*

Mikey   It's complicated.

Carl   If you were stuck in here and I was living it up on the outside I'd come see you every day.

Mikey (*snorts*)   I find that very hard to believe.

Carl   I would! Bring you some fags, a sneaky bit of weed, some Haribo – I'd have to be dragged out at the end of visiting hours.

Mikey (*can't help smiling*)   Sure you would . . .

Etienne *picks up the plate of biscuits from the floor and offers them to* **Mikey**.

Etienne   You sure you don't want a shitty biscuit?

Mikey (*shaking his head adamantly*)   Nah I've got no appetite whatsoever.

Etienne   Troll Face will get angry if I don't hand 'em around.

Carl   I'll have another one.

He leans across and takes a biscuit from the plate.

Etienne *looks from* **Carl** *to* **Mikey**.

Etienne   Your pupils are massive.

Mikey (*hastily*)   No they're not.

Etienne   You tanked up on anti-depressants or something?

Carl (*self-satisfied*)   No actually, we've taken ecstasy.

Mikey   Don't tell him!

Carl   Why not? This is meant to be a fucking party after all.

Etienne (*laughing*)   You lot can't take ecstasy! Won't it make you shrivel up like a ball-sack?

Mikey   No actually it's going pretty well.

Beat.

Etienne (*lowering his voice slightly*)   You got any more?

Carl   Not for you I haven't.

Etienne   I'll pay you. I'm going to a house party later – this girl will be well impressed if I pick up for her.

Carl   Sorry, can't help you.

Etienne   Please, or Joel will get in there first like he always does.

Mikey   You shouldn't need to supply a woman with drugs to get her to like you.

Etienne   Maybe not back in your day, but Jess is a modern woman.

Carl (*to* **Mikey**)   Ali did start fancying me after I gave her free weed.

Mikey   Yeah but then she went out with me – which proves drugs can only get you so far.

Carl   Well I'm the one she married – so I think that proves drugs win.

Mikey (*irritated*)   The only thing you can prove is that you have a shit memory.

Etienne (*interrupting*)   Are you gonna sell me some or not?

Carl   No.

Etienne (*really disappointed*)   But I need some sort of leverage – Joel's a good-looking guy, and he's fuckin' hard.

Carl (*snorts*)   What just like you you mean?

Etienne   Nah he's way harder than me – he breaks into flash cars and drives girls around. They *love* that shit – he gets his dick sucked all the time.

Carl (*to* **Mikey**)   He sounds like a criminal mastermind to me.

Etienne   He is! If he was here he'd put you straight – tell you some stories.

Mikey   Why isn't he here? (*Slight smile.*) I thought you both got arrested for cutting up pensioners?

Etienne *rolls his eyes.*

Etienne   Funny! You know I was lying about that.

Carl   Well what d'you do then?

Etienne (*shaking his head in disbelief*)   I couldn't believe it – the one time he takes me along for the ride and a fucking police car spots us. Joel was right – I should never have worn that yellow hat.

Carl   Classic error.

Etienne   Anyway I had to say it was just me who did it – they would have sent him to Ashfield for sure.

Carl *and* **Mikey** *glance at each other and then burst into laughter.*

Etienne (*offended*)   What?

Carl   Your mate got lucky with you didn't he – you're a fucking idiot!

Etienne (*defensive*)   No I'm not.

Mikey   So he's out having sex in flash cars and you're in here wiping old men's arses?

Carl (*laughs*)   That's brilliant! (*To* **Mikey**.) I should have tried that trick on you.

Etienne   Oi it wasn't no trick, I wanted to help him out . . . Anyway I'm gonna get way more girls now I'm a car thief.

Mikey   But you're not actually a car thief are you?

Etienne   Yeah well they won't know that will they.

Carl (*with a mischievous look at* **Mikey**)   I can't imagine having a best mate I looked up to – you were *so lame*.

Mikey (*defensive*)   I was cooler than you.

Carl   No you weren't! You never stayed up past six in the morning – turning down lines 'cos you 'didn't want to feel too bad on Monday'.

Etienne *looks from one old man to the other as they bicker like kids.*

Mikey   Just 'cos I could moderate my drug taking doesn't mean I was lame.

Carl   Yes it does.

Mikey (*annoyed*)   Why did Ali go out with me then if I was so boring?

Carl   I've already told you – she was shallow. (*Teasing.*) But she soon realised that I was the one who could make her laugh, satisfy her sexually /

Mikey (*interrupting/annoyed*)   Yeah you tell yourself that.

Carl   Don't get mad – it's not my fault you can't handle the truth.

Mikey (*snorts*)   The truth my arse!

Etienne (*frustrated*)   If you're not selling me any then I'm gonna go finish handing out these shitty biscuits before I get in trouble.

Carl *takes a deep breath, taking his time over his answer to leave* **Etienne** *in suspense.*

Carl   OK I'll sell you *one* pill if you go get some of our tunes from our room so we can liven up this party.

Etienne (*jumps up from his chair*)   Deal! (*About to head off stage.*) Hang on I'm gonna need two pills so me and Jess can take them together.

Carl   Oh no you don't wanna do that – you want to be sober so you can take advantage of her properly.

Etienne (*frowning as he wanders off stage*)   I didn't think of that . . .

Mikey (*calling after him*)   Don't listen to him – he's messing with you!

Etienne *exits.*

There is a second of uncomfortable silence.

Carl   I'm sorry I said you were lame.

Mikey (*sulky*)   S'alright . . .

Carl   Listen I know part of the reason you don't feel like hanging around is 'cos you're a bit disappointed with the way things turned out for you. But you've gotta realise it's not a big deal – most people think their lives are shit.

Mikey (*annoyed*)   You're kinda ruining my vibe here.

Carl   I'm just saying it's all about perspective. Think how disappointed Troll Face must be with every single aspect of her life – but she still manages to start each day with a smile.

Mikey (*challenging him*)   Are you disappointed by anything?

Carl   'Course I am.

Mikey (*testing*)   Like what?

Carl *has to think for a moment.*

Carl   I can't really remember what sex was like with Ali . . .
Can you?

Mikey (*nods assertively*)   Yeah – very clearly.

Carl *looks concerned for a second.*

Carl   She loved a good flirt – I remember that much. I'd
watch her across the room at a party chatting to some
chump – gently squeezing his arm as she laughed. I'm sure
she cheated on me. There was this guy she talked about a lot
from her hospital. One of those dicks with the prettyboy
faces /

Mikey   When it's hard to tell if it's a guy or a girl.

Carl   Exactly! And he was brainy – obviously, being a
doctor, but really smug and in your face about it. No beer-
and-curry belly either. He was basically a complete cunt. And
while I was being humiliated you were shagging your way
through the best-looking fanny in Bristol.

Mikey   I really wasn't.

Carl   What was that hot girl called? The blonde you were
with for a while.

Mikey   I never went out with blondes – weren't my type.

Carl   Yes you did! You must remember her – she had a
pleasingly round face, very cute.

Mikey   I dunno who you're talking about.

Carl   And an even rounder arse – even cuter – always wore
black jeans.

Mikey*'s eyes flash with recognition.*

Mikey   You're thinking of Debbie Robinson.

Carl   Debbie! How could I forget.

Mikey   I never went out with her.

Carl (*conceding*)   Alright you had a casual 'friends who fuck occasionally' thing going on or whatever you want to call it.

Mikey *is about to disagree but* **Carl** *gets in there first.*

Carl   Look who's turned up.

Carl *has sat up in his wheelchair, eyes fixed on the opposite side of the room.*

Mikey   They both look nice don't they?

Carl   I suppose Michelle's outfit's alright. But why the hell is Kelly wearing *fishnet tights*? I'm gonna have nightmares for weeks.

He yells across the room.

Carl   Oi Michelle!

Mikey (*loud whisper*)   What are you doing!

Carl (*raising his arm above his head*)   Michelle, over here!

Mikey   Don't you dare!

Carl (*indicating* **Mikey**)   My mate Mikey would really like to f /

Mikey *manages to lean across and twist* **Carl***'s nipple.*

Mikey   Shut up!

Carl   Our! (*Pushing* **Mikey***'s hand away, jovial.*) Come on when was the last time you had sex with a real woman?

Mikey   None of your business.

Carl   Not for ages then.

Mikey *frowns, not wanting to admit he's right.*

Carl   I'm just saying I think it's a shame for you to leave without getting your nuts in one last time. If you really want I'll ask Kelly out too and we can double up – even though I'll probably need trauma counselling afterwards.

Mikey   It's too late for all that.

Carl   No it's not! Think of that glimmer of hope in her eyes.

Mikey   They do sparkle, especially when she wears that green eyeliner.

Carl   And how her tits probably look less terrifying than anyone else's in here.

Mikey   I'd say that was a fact.

Carl *smiles, delighted with his progress.*

Carl   The four of us could take over that corner over there –we'd be like a gang.

Mikey (*voice tinged with excitement*)   That does sound pretty cool . . .

Carl (*enticing*)   See you don't really wanna leave do you? You want to be in a gang and cop a feel of Michelle's tits.

Mikey (*surprised by this revelation*)   I *do* want to be in a gang and cop a feel of Michelle's tits.

Carl (*triumphant*)   So you'll stay!

Mikey *suddenly realises what he's saying, forcing himself to shake his head assertively.*

Mikey   No Carl, I really can't.

Carl *glances at him sulkily.*

Carl   Sarah's going to be upset when she finds you've left me here all by myself.

Mikey   Something tells me Sarah will understand.

Carl   Why don't you just wait till she comes back for Christmas? She could take us out somewhere.

Carl *suddenly becomes excited by this idea, feeling he's latched on to one final way of convincing* **Mikey** *to stay.*

Carl   We could get her to drive us round the Forest of Dean! Remember you were gonna move there.

Mikey   That wasn't me.

Carl   Yes it was! While you were running Clockwork you'd always bang on about wanting to wake up and sniff the fresh forest air, and forget about the millions of fags you'd smoked and all those nasty powders you'd shoved up your nostrils.

Mikey   You're thinking of someone else.

Carl *looks confused for a moment.*

Etienne *enters with the remote from their bedroom. He points it at the tannoy and their grimy dance music blares out across the room.*

Carl (*grinning*)   That's more like it.

Mikey   Finally!

Carl   You should get Michelle to wheel herself over here – you can wave your arms about together.

Etienne *enters and sits back down on the plastic chair.*

Etienne   This isn't actually that bad.

Troll Face *rushes in, turning the music off with the remote control.*

Troll Face (*irritated*)   Who put that on?

Carl *and* **Mikey** *subtly point at* **Etienne**.

Carl   We begged him to turn it off but he wouldn't listen.

Etienne (*crosses his arms*)   I'm not rising to it.

Troll Face *checks the schedule – surprised by how late it is. She moves briskly behind* **Carl**'s *wheelchair, trying to push him off stage.*

Troll Face   OK Carl, time for your bath.

Carl (*jamming the wheels*)   Mikey's leaving soon.

Mikey   I'm not gonna go anywhere till you get back.

Troll Face *tries to push* **Carl** *off stage but he continues to jam the wheels.*

Troll Face (*with a forced smile*)   It won't take long.

Carl   I'm not missing the end of the party.

Troll Face   Stop being difficult.

Carl's *face reddens as he uses all his strength to stop her pushing him off stage.*

Carl   I want to ring my daughter.

He tries to conceal the onset of another headache but he can't help wincing in pain.

Troll Face *takes out the tub of pills from her pocket, tipping one into her hand.*

Troll Face   You need to stop fighting me Carl – you're just making yourself worse.

Carl (*mumbling through the pain*)   Piss off.

Troll Face *bends over* **Carl**, *the pill in her hand.*

Troll Face   Just open your mouth.

Carl *pushes* **Troll Face** *away from him forcefully.*

This act of defiance clearly angers **Troll Face** – *she advances towards him.*

Troll Face   I've really had enough of your attitude.

She uses all her strength to stuff the pill into his mouth.

Mikey (*alarmed*)   Don't force him.

Troll Face (*to* **Etienne**)   Hand me the jug.

Etienne *watches* **Carl** *squirming.*

Troll Face   Now!

Etienne *reluctantly hands her the jug.*

Troll Face *manages to squeeze* **Carl**'s *mouth open and pour some water inside – but it mainly spills all over his face.*

Troll Face (*slightly out of breath*)   There you go that wasn't too bad was it.

Carl *spits out the pill and water all over* **Troll Face**.

Troll Face (*flash of real anger*)   Carl!

She wipes the water off her uniform.

Troll Face (*riled*)   If you stopped being a pain in the arse for one minute you'd realise I was just trying to make your life a little bit more bearable.

Carl *looks at his trainers, a little boy being told off by his mum.*

Troll Face *hands the tub of pills to* **Mikey**.

Troll Face   You can have a go – I've given up.

Carl *meets* **Troll Face**'*s contemptuous look – she's really had enough of him.*

Troll Face *starts to make her way off stage.*

Troll Face (*to* **Etienne**)   Bring him along to the bathroom if he changes his mind – if not he can stink for a week.

She exits.

Carl *can't help watching her go.*

Mikey *stares at* **Carl**, *who is clearly still in pain. He tries to hand him the tub of pills.*

Mikey   Just take 'em will you.

Carl *looks at the tub for a second, before reaching out to take them.*

Etienne   What d'you want to do about this bath then?

Carl (*sadly*)   Let's just get it over with.

Mikey *watches guiltily as* **Etienne** *wheels* **Carl** *off stage.*

Blackout.

6

16.59.58

Carl *and* **Mikey**'*s room.* **Mikey** *is still in his wheelchair, thoughtful and morose. The toy dog sits on the plastic chair. The* **Woman with Red Hair** *is turned away from us slightly so we can't really see her face.*

Woman with Red Hair   Are you sure you're all packed?
Remember it's not like you can just pop back if you forget
anything.

Mikey   I better double check.

The **Woman with Red Hair** *watches as* **Mikey** *rummages through
his bag anxiously.*

Woman with Red Hair   Are you OK?

Mikey   Just making sure I've got everything.

Mikey *takes a photograph out of his rucksack and puts it in the
pocket of his Adidas jumper for safekeeping.*

Woman with Red Hair   I know this is difficult, but aren't
you at least a tiny bit excited?

Mikey (*half-hearted*)   I am excited . . .

Woman with Red Hair   You'll love it there, I promise. The
sun's always shining. There's more food than you could
possibly eat. It will just feel like you've gone on a really
long holiday.

Mikey   A holiday I can't ever come home from.

Woman with Red Hair   There's nothing else you can do.

Mikey   I know . . .

Woman with Red Hair   He'll be OK without you.

Mikey   He'll be lonely.

Woman with Red Hair   You shouldn't feel guilty.

Mikey *looks at his trainers – he knows what he's about to say will
make her angry.*

Mikey   I just thought maybe I could join you in a week
or two.

The **Woman with Red Hair** *shakes her head in disbelief – she
should have seen this coming.*

Woman with Red Hair   I can't believe he can still make you do *exactly* what he wants.

Mikey   Can we talk about this downstairs – he'll be back any minute.

Woman with Red Hair   We're leaving *now*.

Mikey   I just want to say goodbye to him properly, make sure he's made some new friends.

Woman with Red Hair   What about this weekend? Josh was going to take us out on his boat.

Mikey (*trying not to sound too impressed*)   Josh has a boat?

Woman with Red Hair (*persuasive*)   In a couple of days you could be sunbathing out on the deck with nothing for miles but clear blue sea.

Mikey *considers this enticing prospect for a moment.*

Woman with Red Hair *smiles, pleased she's winning him over.*

Woman with Red Hair   It'll be just like that time in France.

Carl *is wheeled into the room by* **Troll Face**. *He doesn't notice the* **Woman with Red Hair** *for a second as* **Troll Face** *has to negotiate his wheelchair through the door.*

Troll Face (*awkward*)   We interrupting something?

Mikey'*s face falls – this is exactly what he wanted to avoid.*

Mikey   That was a quick bath . . .

Carl (*shocked*)   Sarah?

Carl *wheels himself nearer* **Sarah**.

Carl   What are you doing here?

Mikey *doesn't know what to say.*

Sarah (*to* **Troll Face**)   Can you tell the taxi we'll be down in a minute?

Troll Face (*awkward*)   Of course.

Troll Face *exits.*

Carl (*to* **Mikey**, *confused*)   Why didn't you tell me Sarah was taking you to the clinic?

Mikey (*lying badly*)   I forgot . . .

Carl   You forgot?! I didn't even know she was in the country.

Mikey (*stares at his trainers guiltily*)   I'm sorry . . .

Sarah *puts a firm hand on* **Mikey**'s *shoulder.*

Sarah (*brisk*)   Why don't you say your goodbyes?

Carl   Hold on a minute.

Mikey *is just about to speak but* **Sarah** *gets in there first.*

Sarah (*to* **Carl**)   I'm sorry but we really have to go.

Mikey   We can stay a bit longer can't we?

Sarah (*annoyed, to* **Mikey**)   I can't believe you're doing this – you promised.

Mikey   Five minutes – it's the least we can do.

Sarah (*impatient*)   It's a Saturday, it'll take us ages to get through customs.

Mikey *glares at* **Sarah** *– she's just made the situation a lot worse.*

Carl (*looking around at her slowly*)   You're going to the airport?

Sarah   Yes Carl we're /

Mikey (*interrupting*)   Don't – I'll tell him.

Carl (*confused and frustrated*)   Tell me what?!'

Mikey *is silent for a moment, his resolve breaking.*

Mikey (*very guilty*)   I don't have a brain tumour . . .

Carl *is momentarily speechless, reeling from shock. He suddenly becomes animated.*

Carl I knew it! I fucking knew it.

Mikey And I'm not going to a clinic.

Carl You lying bastard.

Mikey (*guilty*) I'm moving in with Sarah and her fiancé.

Carl (*turning to* **Sarah**) Why is he moving in with you?

Sarah You've left him no choice.

Carl (*confused*) I've been trying to make him stay. (*To* **Mikey**.) Haven't I?

Mikey (*tentative*) Carl how much can you remember about your relationship with Ali?

Carl's eyes flash angrily, something inside him suddenly resentful.

Carl What kind of question's that?

Mikey What can you actually remember?

Carl (*defensive*) Lots of things . . . Her green and yellow trainers. The way her eyes looked when she flirted with me.

Mikey But what about the first time you had sex? Or how it felt to put the ring on her finger?

Carl becomes flustered.

Carl I don't like the way you're talking to me.

Mikey That's rich coming from you.

Carl (*defensive*) What's that meant to mean?

Mikey You did always love taking the piss out of me. A dig about how skinny I was, or how I was such a prettyboy it was hard to tell if I was a guy or a girl.

Carl I never said that.

Mikey I didn't really mind, it was no worse than the stuff guys usually say to each other – till me and Ali got together. Glastonbury 2008 was a standout festival – you got so drunk you *accidentally* unzipped my tent in the middle of the night and pissed all over me. And then you told everyone we knew as if it was some hilarious story.

Carl   I thought it was a portaloo!

Mikey   What about our lads' holiday in Amsterdam – when you almost drove our pedalo into an oncoming boat just to make me think we were gonna die?

Carl   You have to admit that was fun.

Mikey   And force feeding me hash cake till I was sick. That was fun too was it?

Carl (*defiant*)   Yes, it was.

Mikey's *eyes narrow, momentarily bitter.*

Mikey   You can't remember what the sex was like with Ali 'cos you never actually had sex with her. I don't think you even ever held her hand.

Carl *is silent for a short moment, taking in this shocking claim.*

Carl (*forcing a smile*)   That's really funny that is. You've finally developed a sense of humour.

Mikey   I'm not joking Carl.

Carl (*another forced smile*)   I was married to her.

Mikey   No you weren't, I was.

Carl *laughs to disguise his complete confusion.*

Carl (*indicating* **Sarah**)   So I guess that would mean she's your daughter?

Sarah (*really awkward*)   I am . . .

Carl *grins and shakes his head – but we can sense his uncertainty growing.*

Carl   I knew it was April Fools' Day.

Sarah *sits down on the plastic chair, finding the situation very hard to deal with.*

Mikey   Don't you think it's a bit weird you can remember her trainers but you can't remember your wedding day?

Carl   I was hammered.

Mikey   Yeah you were – 'cos you left halfway through the service so you could drink all the booze before anyone got to the reception and then you passed out in the toilets covered in your own vomit.

Carl   I would never do such a thing. (*He shakes his head vigorously but we can tell he's confused.*) That's definitely not what happened. I've passed out in toilets on loads of occasions – you must be thinking of one of them.

Mikey   Didn't you ever wonder why I took down all my photos?

Carl   That was your business.

Mikey   When you first noticed our wedding photo you completely froze – as if it was an alien object you should never have come in contact with. That was the first time I realised you were seriously confused.

Carl   Can you hear yourself?

Mikey   You've never been to Japan – that wasn't your honeymoon.

Carl (*increasingly worried*)   Stop being such a prick!

Sarah (*to* **Carl**)   You brought this on yourself.

Carl   I haven't done anything!

Mikey   Sarah's friend works for the Alzheimer's Institute. You're on their system Carl. I'm not angry with you, but those microchips were designed to help you kepp hold of your own memories, not so you can just upload whatever you want on to it . . . if you think about what you did, it's essentially identity theft.

Carl (*shakes his head in disbelief*)   You're insane.

Mikey   I guess after Ali's funeral you thought we'd probably never see each other again.

Carl *suddenly lifts his head up, defiant.*

Carl   You just can't handle the fact she loved someone like me.

Mikey   She did love you, at one point – I knew that . . . But you never actually told her how you felt.

Carl (*aggravated*)   I told her exactly how I felt. D'you want me to tell you what happened? 'Cos you won't like it.

Mikey   Try me.

Sarah (*losing patience*)   Dad we don't have time.

Mikey   I just need a couple more minutes, I promise.

Sarah *starts pacing anxiously.*

Carl *launches in confidently – he knows he's remembering this part correctly.*

Carl   OK so we were at Clockwork, in that alcove on the second floor where we all used to hang out when we were kids.

Mikey   Stoners' corner.

Carl   I even rolled us a cheeky spliff . . . Then she said you'd asked her to marry you. I felt sick. And I knew I had to say something – there was unfinished business between us. Some things are just meant to happen. Like they're planned out before you're born. So if you don't act on them then lots of the other shit that's meant to happen to you might not happen either. So I thought about this and I told her . . . I said . . .

Carl *desperately tries to salvage what's left of the memory, his eyes beginning to gleam with fear.*

Carl   You wanted me to think you were dead – do you know how sick that is? D'you hate me that much?

Mikey 'Course not! We've had fun over the last few months – but if we carry on like this we'll drive each other mad.

Carl *remains silent, brain racing furiously.*

Sarah'*s mobile phone starts ringing, she retrieves it from her pocket and answers it.*

Sarah Thank you, we're coming. (*Hanging up.*) Dad we need to leave.

Mikey Not until he believes me.

Sarah He's never going to.

Carl (*quiet*) She's right Mikey – just piss off.

Mikey I can't go if he thinks I hate him.

Sarah Don't let him manipulate you.

Mikey Can you wait for me in the taxi? I won't be long.

Sarah Dad if we don't go now /

Mikey If we miss the plane we miss the fucking plane.

Sarah (*had enough*) Fine, do what you want.

She starts to move off stage – she suddenly stops and turns back to **Carl**, *softening for a second.*

Sarah Bye Carl.

She exits.

Carl *watches her go.*

Carl *and* **Mikey** *are finally alone.* **Carl** *looks utterly exhausted, his brain is too tired to take anything else in.*

Mikey You must be able to remember something.

Carl Why haven't you left already?

Mikey You lost a bit of weight after our wedding – does that ring a bell?

Carl (*pretends not to be interested*) Did I . . .?

Mikey   Made an effort to move on – even started seeing a nice girl called Debbie Robinson.

Carl (*snorts*)   You're not gonna convince me of that one.

Mikey   But when you and Debbie came round to see Sarah for the first time it was painfully obvious nothing had changed. You could barely bring yourself to look at her.

Carl *is incredibly concerned and disorientated, the memory beginning to re-emerge.*

Carl   Mikey I'm tired, I just wanna be left /

Mikey (*carrying straight on*)   I couldn't help watching as Ali kissed you goodbye. She let her face rest against yours, and I swear for a second you were teenagers again.

Carl *is silent for a long moment. The room is incredibly quiet and still.*

Carl   I remember that.

Mikey *exhales deeply, but he feels no sense of relief.*

Mikey   I thought you might.

Desperate for a distraction, **Carl** *wheels himself over to the dog lying on the plastic chair, picking it up.*

Carl   She never cheated on me – that was you.

Beat.

Mikey   You ran Clockwork for a few years.

Carl (*nods*)   Makes sense I suppose. (*Snorts.*) Certainly more sense than you running it square boy.

Mikey   Sometimes I'd bump into you on Stokes Croft on a Sunday afternoon. I'd be on my way for a roast and you'd still be up from the night before – tell-tale ring of powder round the nostrils, pupils so huge they could barely fit in your eyes. One time I thought I should say something – point out that you were over forty, maybe it was time to slow down. Look into forestry conservation like you'd always talked about.

Carl Bet I loved that.

Mikey I didn't see you again for over twenty years – till Ali's funeral. You were very vague about what you'd been up to. Talked a lot about wanting to move in here though, when the time was right – gave me the impression it would be far more luxurious!

Carl I remember the funeral – it was raining wasn't it?

Mikey Yeah.

Carl But everyone was wearing these really bright colours, 'cos that's what she'd asked for in her will. She always had to be unconventional.

Mikey (*smiles knowingly*) She married me in a red and black dress.

There's a moment of silence.

Carl Can I see it?

Mikey What?

Carl The wedding photo.

Mikey *takes the photograph out of the pocket of his jumper, handing it to* **Carl**.

Carl She looks so much like Sarah.

Carl *forces himself to look at the photograph for an extended moment.*

Carl *nods as he hands back the photo, finally conceding.*

Carl (*with a smile*) You were a lucky bastard.

Mikey Yeah, I was.

Mikey's *mobile phone rings from inside his pocket.*

Mikey That'll be Sarah.

He takes the phone out and cancels the call.

Carl You better go.

Mikey (*still uncertain*)   I guess . . .

There is a second of awkward silence, neither of them wanting
Mikey *to leave yet.*

Mikey's *phone starts ringing again.*

Mikey. Jesus, I'm coming.

He turns the phone off, rolling his eyes.

Mikey *extends his hand for* **Carl** *to shake.*

Mikey   Bye Carl.

Carl *shakes his hand.*

Mikey *pauses for a second, still unsure he's doing the right thing,*
before finally starting to wheel himself off stage.

Carl   Mikey.

Mikey *turns his body to face* **Carl.**

Carl   I'm sorry.

Mikey   Me too.

Mikey *continues to wheel himself off stage, he calls back to* **Carl** *as*
he disappears.

Mikey   And give old Kelly a chance.

Carl   That aborted foetus? I'd rather /

But **Mikey** *has gone before* **Carl** *can finish his sentence.*

There is complete silence for a short moment.

Etienne *enters, eyeing* **Carl**'s *sad figure cautiously.*

Etienne   You alright?

Carl   Never better.

Etienne *stands there awkwardly, unsure how to phrase the question.*

Etienne   Um, I just wondered if I could get that pill off you
– my shift's finished so . . .

Carl *takes the boiled sweet tin out of the pocket of his Adidas jumper and hands it to* **Etienne**.

Carl   Take 'em all.

Etienne (*opening the tin, surprised*)   Really?

Carl (*forcing a sad smile*)   No use having drugs if you've got no one to share them with.

Etienne *looks down at the sweet tin – he knows he should be delighted to have this precious commodity but the whole situation feels too depressing.*

Etienne   Cheers . . . if this doesn't get me laid I don't know what will.

He exits awkwardly.

Carl *is left on stage by himself.*

Fade to black.

7

13.55.00

Carl *is sitting in a wheelchair, sweating under the bright lights in his Adidas hooded jumper. He looks pale and sickly.* **Troll Face** *and* **Etienne** *are sitting on plastic chairs on either side of him. They are all wearing Christmas hats and holding slices of Christmas cake on paper party plates.*

There is a faint sound of children singing carols and people chatting.

Carl *looks extremely unimpressed.*

Carl   When are they taking the children away?

Troll Face   You're not enjoying it?

Carl (*as if she's insane*)   No . . .

Troll Face   They've taken time out of their Saturday to come here and sing for you.

Etienne   They're rubbish.

Troll Face   Don't be cruel. Look at their little angelic faces.

Carl   The faces of death.

Troll Face   Carl!

Carl *surveys the room.*

Carl (*to* **Etienne**)   How would you rate this party on a scale of 1 to 10?

Etienne (*thinks about it seriously*)   About a minus 5.

Troll Face (*through mouthfuls*)   It's not that bad! There's cake.

Etienne   It's nothing compared to where I was at last night that's for sure.

Carl   Let me guess . . . you stayed in by yourself wanking?

Etienne   No! . . . Not last night – went to Jess's party didn't I?

Carl   Ah the famous Jess. I can't believe fifteen pills weren't enough to get you in her pants. That girl's hard to please.

Etienne   Tell me about it. I had a bit more luck last night though.

Carl   Yeah right.

Etienne   I did! I told her if she'd rather get off with Joel than with me then she's a dumb bitch.

Troll Face   How did that go down?

Etienne   She thought I was being rude. (*Pretends he's not being genuine.*) Had to backtrack and say he wasn't good enough for her and all this other soppy bullshit.

Troll Face   That's actually quite sweet.

Etienne   I'll tell you what was sweet – her fanny juice.

Carl   Like you got a taste.

Etienne (*conceding*)   Not yet.

He grins as he stands up.

Etienne   But soon . . .

He takes off his party hat and leaves it on top of the chair with the rest of his cake.

Etienne (*to* **Carl**)   Guess this is it cripple.

Carl   You're a free man.

Carl *retrieves the porn magazine from behind his back.*

Carl   You better have this – you're gonna need something to wank over when that girl breaks your heart.

Etienne *looks down at the porn magazine as if it's the nicest gift anyone's ever given him.*

Etienne   I don't know what to say.

Carl (*jovial*)   Just fuck off before I change my mind.

Etienne *has a distinct spring in his step as he exits, calling behind him.*

Etienne   See ya Troll Face.

Troll Face (*calling after him*)   That's not my name!

Troll Face *glances at her watch. She takes out the tub of pills from her pocket and hands it to* **Carl** *with a plastic cup of water.*

Carl *takes a pill out of the tub and swallows it down with a gulp of water.*

Carl   I can't believe they didn't tell me that stupid chip could give me a brain tumour – I'm gonna sue.

Troll Face   I thought they did tell you there was a risk?

Carl   Yeah, a *very small* one. Apparently I'm a particularly unusual case.

Troll Face   That's pretty unfortunate.

Troll Face *takes out a packet of cigarettes, she hands one to* **Carl** *and then lights one herself.*

Carl (*with a smile*)   I can't believe you're not trying to convince me to stay – anyone would think you'd had enough of me.

Troll Face   I just know I'd make the same choice – I'd much rather die in a clinic than in here. (*Hastily.*) But if you're having doubts you should /

Carl (*interrupting*)   Nah, it's definitely the right time . . .

Carl *enjoys breathing in the nicotine.*

Carl   I can't believe that skinny bastard is going to outlive me. He was the one who had flu every winter. Runny eyes in the summer 'cos of his *hay fever*. Natural selection should have bumped him off years ago.

Troll Face   He is living in California, he has an unfair advantage.

Carl   Yeah it'll be all that real chicken he's eating.

Troll Face   If it makes you feel any better I'm sure Mikey's time isn't too far off.

Carl   Thanks Troll Face. I always knew you had a kind heart beneath that terrifying exterior.

Troll Face   Cheers . . .

Carl   Turns out I had a bit of money saved that I'd forgotten about – not a huge sum, but not a pathetic amount either. I've left it to you in the will.

Troll Face *slowly swallows her mouthful of cake, genuinely shocked.*

Troll Face   But what about your family – or Mikey?

Carl   He wouldn't take it.

Troll Face   But there must be someone else you hate less than me.

Carl *shakes his head, surprised.*

Carl   No actually there isn't. (*Wry smile.*) Maybe I've got Stockholm syndrome.

Troll Face (*with a smile*)   I can't think of any other explanation.

Carl   I was gonna say I'd like you to put the money into the home – make it a bit nicer for the other residents. But to be honest I don't give a shit what it's like here after I've gone. In fact I'd prefer it if they're all just as uncomfortable as I was. So spend it on whatever the hell you want, some new slippers or something – go wild.

Troll Face   That's very kind of you Carl, thank you.

Carl   It's alright – it must be pretty shit being a nurse.

Troll Face   D'you know what, it really is. I think I'm gonna pack it in soon.

Carl (*surprised*)   Really?

Troll Face   I just want to try something more relaxing – I reckon being a masseuse would be pretty chilled. I had a go in Thailand, when I wasn't shitting myself, and they told me I was a natural.

Carl   I'm not sure many people will want you to rub oil into their backs with your sausage fingers.

Troll Face   I just hate always rushing around like a maniac – forcing myself to smile while I'm washing an old man's arse-crack.

Carl (*smiling at the memory*)   You always washed mine so thoroughly.

Troll Face   I can't remember the last time I had a moment to just sit down and relax with a shitty magazine – it might be over twenty years. Sometimes I even have fantasies about lying in a hot bath with a copy of *Hello!*. (*Hastily.*) Don't tell my husband – he thinks it's shameful.

Carl   He's the one who should be ashamed – he married you didn't he?

Troll Face (*sarcastic smile*)   I'm really going to miss your sense of humour.

She suddenly notices something on the other side of the room, leaning in closer to **Carl**.

Troll Face   Kelly keeps looking over here. Is she a special friend of yours?

Carl   Special's one word for her.

Troll Face   I think she's giving you a wave.

Carl *doesn't even look in her direction.*

Carl   Nah she'll be giving me the finger. It just takes a while to get fully upright, very similar to /

Troll Face   She's definitely waving.

Carl   She's really not, she's . . .

Carl *squints. He suddenly seems shy and bashful. He raises his hand into an awkward wave, his face unconsciously breaking into a slight smile.*

The CHILDREN'S SINGING becomes even louder, rising in a crescendo.

Blackout.

8

00.00.00

Carl *is dead. He is sitting in a wheelchair wearing his Adidas hooded jumper.* **Ali/Sarah** *walks out of the darkness, she is wearing green and yellow trainers. She is rigid and still like a mannequin.* **Carl** *looks at her in astonishment. He gets out of his wheelchair and walks towards her.*

Carl   Fuck. They really made you.

He stares at her for a moment, before gently poking her arm with his finger.

Carl   You're so soft . . . so real. They've really pushed the boat out with you new models haven't they?

He stares at her blank face, swallowing uncomfortably.

Carl   So, how's life been treating you?

Ali *doesn't even blink.*

Carl   I guess you're not one of the ones that talk eh?

Silence. **Carl** *looks at his hands, unsure how to proceed. He stares at her for a moment.*

Blue lasers flash across the room and non-cheesy dance music starts to play in the background, creating the impression we're in a club.

Carl   D'you remember when we came here to smoke cheeky joints? You used to do this thing with your eyes. Sometimes I thought you wanted me to kiss you, but then I figured I must have a screw loose. You and Mikey were always much better suited, the right fit – we'd have never . . .

Carl *is silent for a second, changing his mind.*

Carl   Listen I know Mikey's a lot better-looking. A lot better at most things. But I've always felt there was something between us – something that won't ever shift unless we see where it goes. I can tell by the way you look at me. By the way you flirt. By the way you get jealous when I'm with other girls even though you've got no fucking right.

Carl   If I'm right about this. If there's even the slightest chance. I'd blow off everyone else I know, I'd even fuck over my best mate – 'cos I love you.

He takes her rigid face in his hands, holding it firmly but not aggressively. He kisses her.

The lifeless **Ali** *remains still as stone.*

Carl   You're not gonna give me anything?

Carl *starts to look concerned.*

Carl   Come on.

Ali *is motionless.*

Carl *grows anxious, gently shaking her shoulder.*

Carl   Please do something.

Carl *grows annoyed, shaking her shoulders a bit more aggressively.*

Carl   Do something.

Carl *looks at her lifeless body – giving up hope. Despite his frustration, he can't help resting his head against hers for a second.*

For a moment **Ali** *doesn't even flinch.*

Suddenly she lifts her arms like a robot, mechanically wrapping them around him.

Carl *smiles with happiness and relief, closing his eyes.*